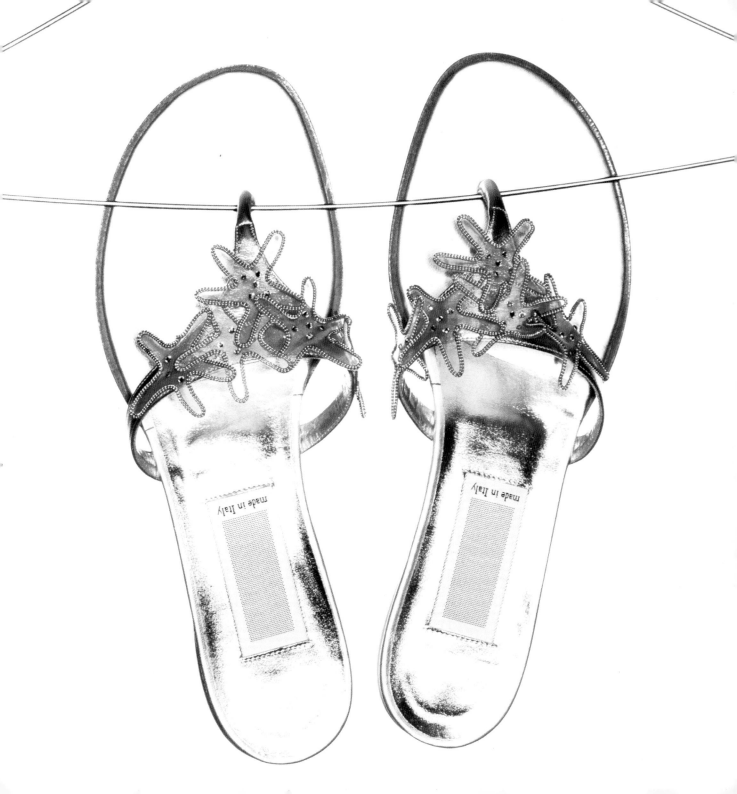

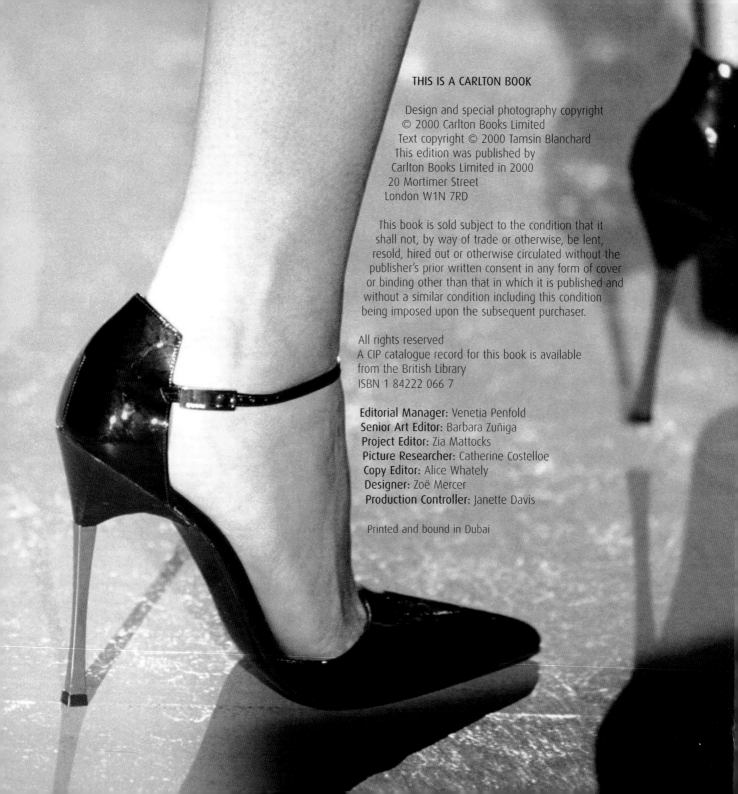

THIS IS A CARLTON BOOK

Design and special photography copyright
© 2000 Carlton Books Limited
Text copyright © 2000 Tamsin Blanchard
This edition was published by
Carlton Books Limited in 2000
20 Mortimer Street
London W1N 7RD

A CIP catalogue record for this book is available
from the British Library
ISBN 1 84222 066 7

Editorial Manager: Venetia Penfold
Senior Art Editor: Barbara Zuñiga
Project Editor: Zia Mattocks
Picture Researcher: Catherine Costelloe
Copy Editor: Alice Whately
Designer: Zoë Mercer
Production Controller: Janette Davis

Printed and bound in Dubai

theshoe

best foot forward

TAMSIN BLANCHARD

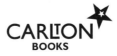

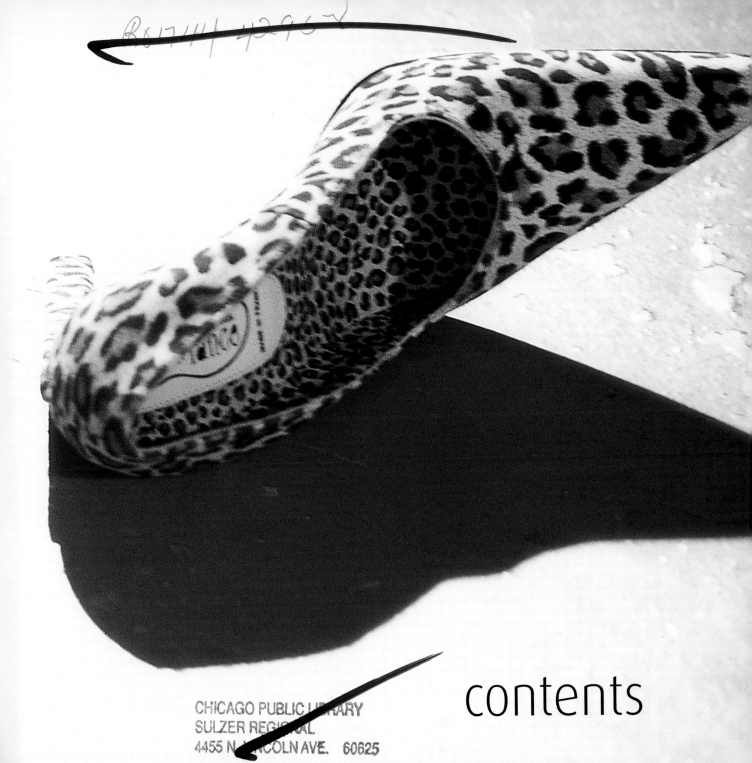

contents

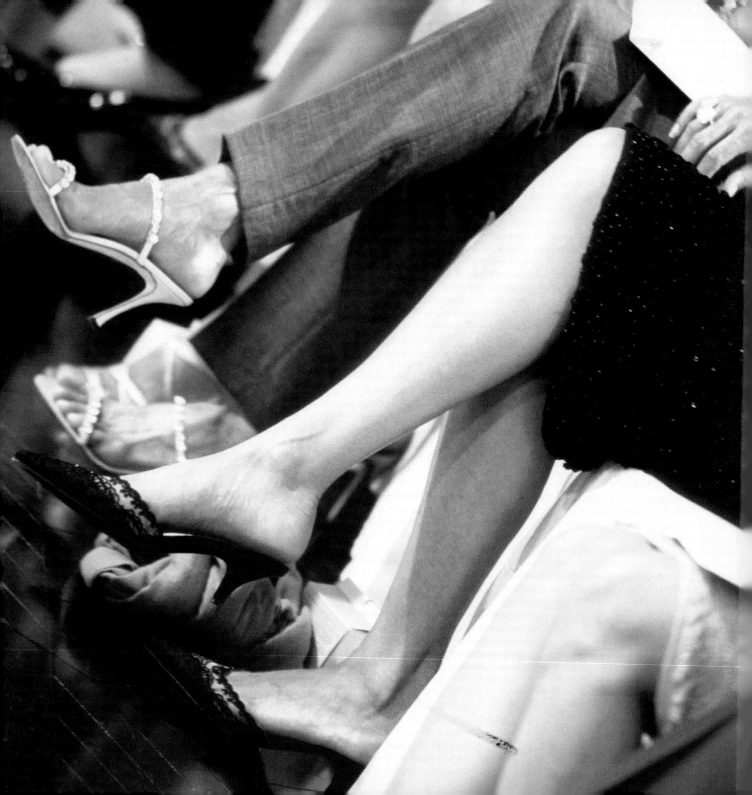

introduction

Far too many times have I taken taxi rides for just a few hundred yards up the road. Taxi drivers swear and curse; the distances have been perfectly walkable. Any relatively healthy person would have happily jogged without so much as breaking into a light sweat. But to walk would have been unthinkable. No, I do not have a bad case of ingrowing toenails. I simply have two close colleagues with whom I have spent many a fashion week who cannot, will not, walk any distance at all, simply because their shoes will not allow it.

Fashion shows are not just an opportunity for designers to show off their collections for the season ahead; they are also the perfect place for fashion reporters, editors, buyers, and groupies to show off their shoes. Scan the front row of any show and you will see the most extraordinary collection of footwear, by some of the grandest shoemakers around. There is American *Vogue*'s Anna Wintour in her bare legs and Manolos, or Kate Betts of *Harper's Bazaar* in the shiny, gravity-defying patent-leather Pradas she bought the day she arrived in Milan. A few seats along, you might see Mimi Spencer of London's *Evening Standard* in a pair of risqué snakeskin spike heels by Sergio Rossi. The fashion cognoscenti are obsessed with haute heels.

Heels are seductive, and no wonder. They elongate the leg and give the foot a really sexy shape. I once saw the model Carla Bruni spend a 40-minute fitting in bare feet, prettily posing on her toes for the entire duration. Just like Barbie, even without shoes, she was wearing imaginary heels.

While I can see the attraction of heels, I am a comfort queen and hate not being able to run, skip, or walk down a street. So although this book is packed with impossible shoe fantasies, and is devoted to my two shoe-obsessed, taxi-bound colleagues, it also offers a few alternatives to those who like to keep their feet a little closer to the ground.

chapter 1
NO **PAIN,** NO **GAIN**

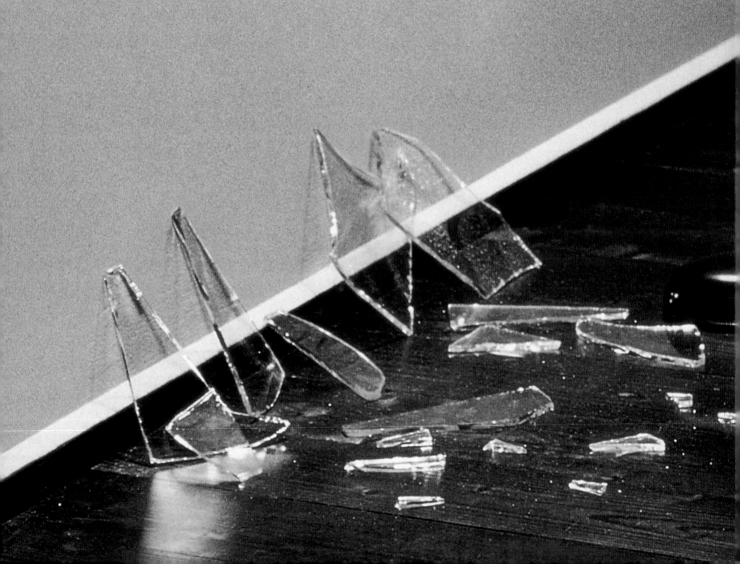

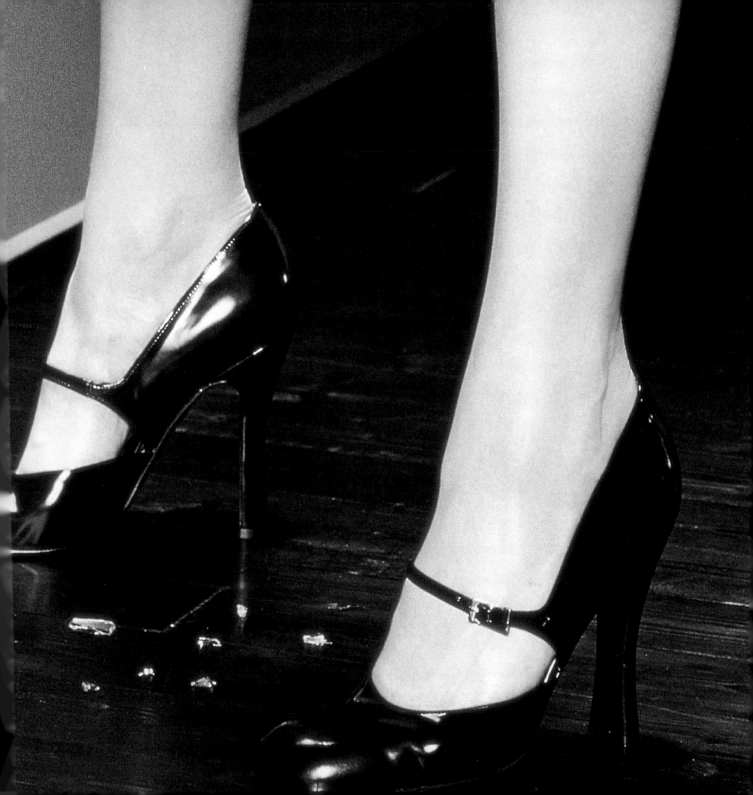

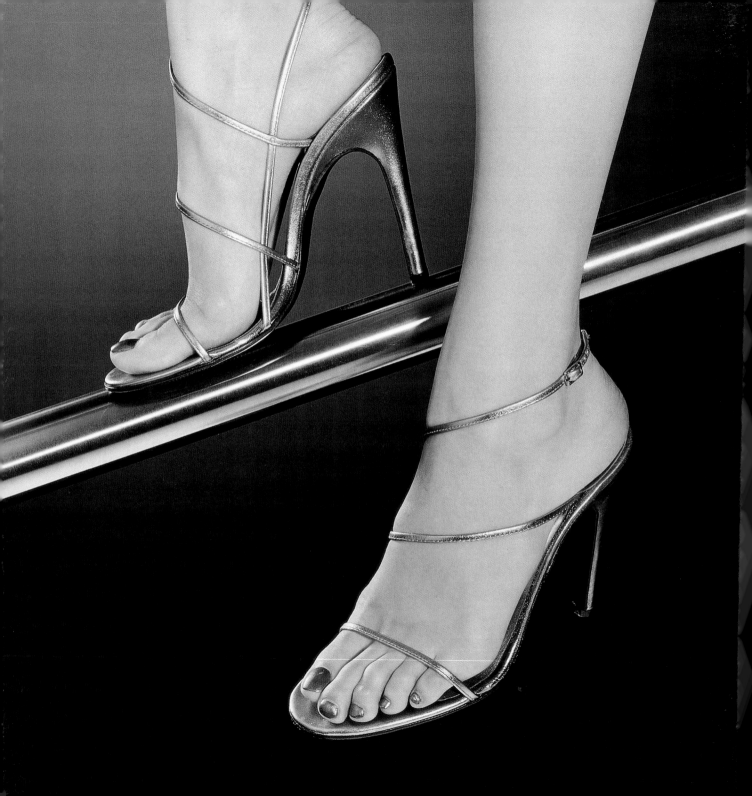

WOMEN HAVE ALWAYS FOUND WAYS OF TORTURING AND DISTORTING THEIR FEET. IN TENTH-CENTURY CHINA, FEET WERE BOUND AND WERE SUPPOSED TO RESEMBLE GOLDEN LILIES IN THEIR TINY, ORNATELY EMBROIDERED SLIPPERS, WHICH WERE DESIGNED PURELY FOR DECORATION. FEET WOULD BE BOUND BETWEEN THE AGES OF THREE AND FIVE, USUALLY TO STUNT THEIR GROWTH TO A DAINTY FIVE INCHES. AS PART OF HER DOWRY, A GIRL WOULD MAKE A SERIES OF SHOES THAT WOULD BE GIVEN AWAY AS PRESENTS TO HER NEW IN-LAWS. THE SMALLER THE FOOT, THE MORE PAMPERED AND WEALTHY THE WOMAN. HER FEET WERE A SYMBOL OF HER STATUS AND MEANT THAT NOT ONLY WOULD SHE NEVER WORK, SHE WOULD NEED A SERVANT TO SUPPORT HER WHEN SHE WALKED. FOOT BINDING WAS FINALLY BANNED IN 1912, BUT IT CONTINUED IN SOME CIRCLES UNTIL THE 1930S. IN THE TWENTY-FIRST CENTURY, IT IS PERHAPS ODD THAT WOMEN—IN BOTH THE EAST AND THE WEST—CONTINUE TO MAKE IT DIFFICULT FOR THEMSELVES TO WALK BY WEARING HIGH HEELS. A SIMILAR PSYCHOLOGY OF WEALTH AND STATUS MAY STILL BE OPERATING; THE RICHER YOU ARE, THE HIGHER THE HEELS, AND THE MORE LIKELY IT IS THAT YOU ONLY HAVE TO WALK A FEW SHORT, PAINFUL STEPS FROM YOUR LIMO TO YOUR DESTINATION.

WALK TALL IN BARELY
THERE STRAPPY HEELS
BY SERGIO ROSSI

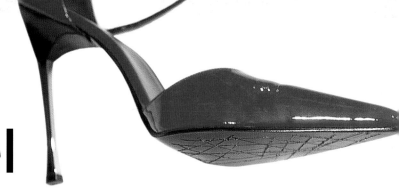

the **rise** of the **heel**

The spike heel came into vogue in the 1950s when a pair of high-heel dress shoes was as essential a part of a woman's wardrobe as her gloves, hat, and handbag—preferably all matching. Roger Vivier is credited with popularizing the "stiletto" heel, thanks to his designs for Christian Dior. Certainly, it was a radical change from the wedge heels of the 1940s. The word stiletto literally means sharp dagger, and it is no coincidence that the heel was adopted by femmes fatales both in real life and on the silver screen. The appeal of the stiletto is the contradiction between its apparent fragility and its hard, siren sex appeal. It adds height, pushing the foot onto its toes and making an exaggerated arch and an elongated calf. There is no denying that the thin, spindly heel flatters the shape of the leg, and a well-made high-heel shoe is supposed to be so expertly engineered that it is comfortable, too.

Shoes with raised heels are by no means a twentieth-century invention, however. Japanese geishas wore wooden geta, which were thonged sandals mounted on two blocks of wood, giving them height and making them walk with a provocative gait. In the 1500s shoes were given extra height by a platform sole called a chopine. They are referred to in Shakespeare's *Hamlet*: "Your ladyship is nearer to heaven than when I saw you last, by the altitude of a chopine." It was during the time of Louis XIV and Marie Antoinette, in seventeenth-century Paris, that the heel (in red if you were a true aristocrat) really

THE LOUIS HEEL SEEMS TAME IN COMPARISON TO TODAY'S SHARP STILETTOS

became a fashion trend, to be continued into the eighteenth century when the footwear and elaborate dress of the French court spread its influence across the rest of Europe. By 1789, however, Josephine Bonaparte was sporting flat shoes. And the most fashionable women across the continent followed suit, wearing their delicate heelless satin slippers with Empire-line dresses to match. But of course, fashion works in reaction to itself, and by the mid-nineteenth century Louis heels were back in vogue.

The twentieth century has seen heel heights fluctuate as often as skirt lengths. In the 1940s they were high and wedge-shaped and in the 1950s high and pointy. In the 1960s there were low kitten heels as well as towering stilettos, most famously fetishized by

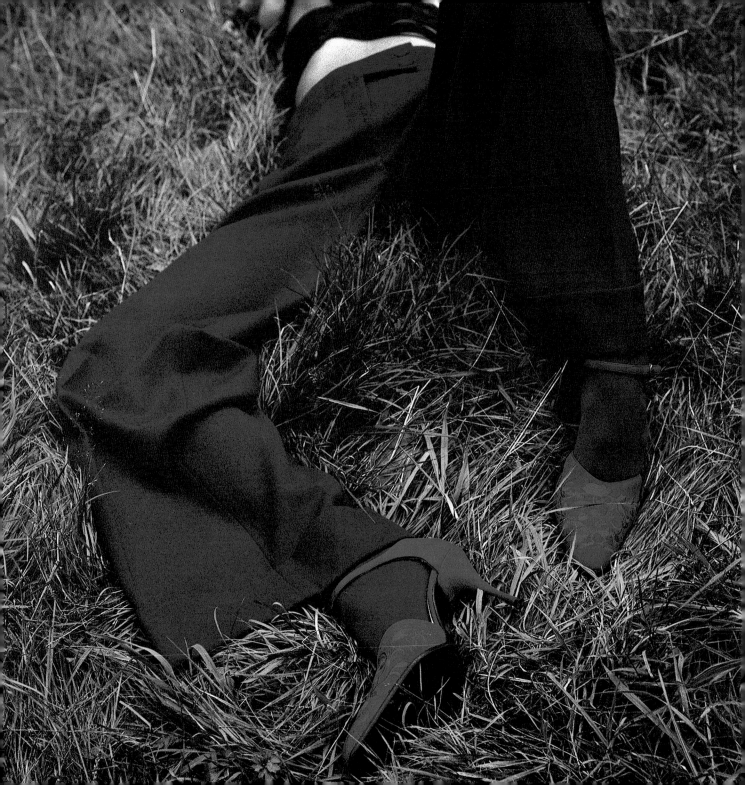

the British pop artist Allen Jones. The 1970s saw a revival of the 1940s wedge and, of course, the rise and rise of the platform, but it is the 1980s that will be forever linked with the stiletto. Short skirts and high heels are a match made in heaven, especially if the wearer wants to flaunt her sex appeal as well as her power. Chanel heels were, literally, the height of postfeminist fashion. The working girl of the 1980s wore high heels in the boardroom as well as the bedroom. White spikes and matching clutch bags became the symbol of a generation of high-powered women. But just like the stock market and property prices, it was all to come crashing to the ground by the end of the decade. The stiletto brigade then took to wearing trainers.

There are some women, however, for whom a high heel is as natural as having ten toes or a leg wax. The ever-fickle world of fashion passes them by as they teeter along on their three-inch spikes without a care in the world. They insist that flat shoes are

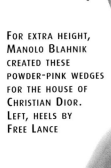

FOR EXTRA HEIGHT, MANOLO BLAHNIK CREATED THESE POWDER-PINK WEDGES FOR THE HOUSE OF CHRISTIAN DIOR. LEFT, HEELS BY FREE LANCE

THE HEEL IS SYNONYMOUS WITH THE DOMINATRIX, HALF SHOE, HALF DEADLY WEAPON, DRAWN HERE BY ALLEN JONES

uncomfortable, and many osteopaths will agree that their feet and the shape of their spines have been irrevocably altered into high-heel mode. Manolo Blahnik began making shoes in 1971. He has always loved a heel and so have his devotees. So the finely tuned fashion eye would say that the high heel is never out of fashion. Certainly, throughout the 1990s, when no one style of shoe, boot, heel, or sole dominated, the most fashionably shod feet have been consistently well-heeled.

Two of the biggest influences on shoes, and fashion itself, have been the phenomenon that is Prada and the rejuvenation of the Gucci label. When Tom Ford rekindled the Gucci flame, he did it with high heels, and every woman who saw them fell instantly in love. Each season, when a new collection is unveiled, shoe fetishists among the assembled crowd of celebrities, press, and buyers crane their necks to see the shape of the shoe and the height of the heel. Ford took the idea of the stiletto one step further by designing metal heels—adding a dangerous frisson by implying that the stilettos could really be used to stab someone in the back.

FINE STRAPS—AND THE RIGHT CHOICE OF STOCKINGS— ADD TO THE ALLURE OF THE HIGH HEEL

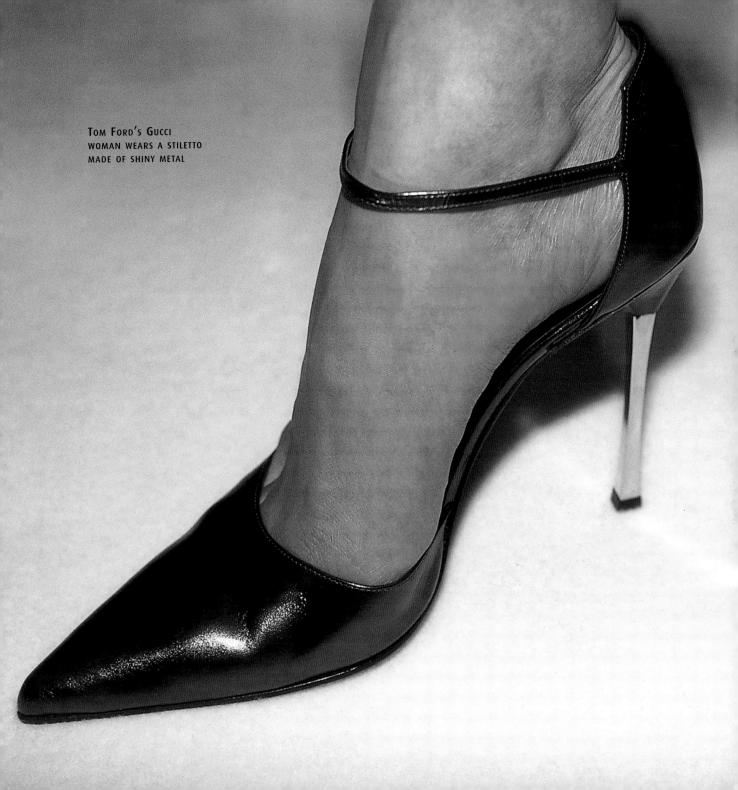

TOM FORD'S GUCCI
WOMAN WEARS A STILETTO
MADE OF SHINY METAL

flat feet

W hat goes up must come down. And even the most foolhardy of heel wearers must have a day off once in a while. There are many women, however, who very rarely—if ever— scale the dizzy heights of a two- or three-inch heel. They are much happier on the flat. That is not to say that they do not love their shoes, but just that they love their feet, too. Flat shoes are associated with sensible shoes, but the two do not always go together. Take flip-flops. They are not exactly the most comfortable,

FLAT SHOES DO NOT HAVE TO BE SENSIBLE SHOES. A FLAT SANDAL CAN BE JUST AS DELICATE AND STRAPPY AS A HIGH ONE

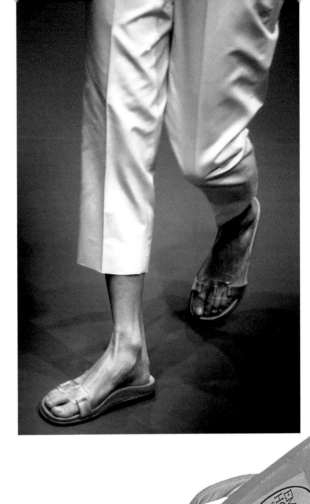

or sensible, of shoe designs, with their single
thong pushed rudely between two toes,
holding the entire sole onto the foot. But
in their roughest and most common form,
they are the perfect cheap sandals for a beach
vacation. They have also been adopted by
certain shoe designers as the basis for
summer sandals, often fancy ones at that.
Jimmy Choo has made flip-flops with a single
flower sprouting between the toes, while
Emma Hope's are fit for an Indian princess.

Occasionally, flat shoes come into fashion. For example, with their
gangster look of the late 1980s Dolce e Gabbana made men's
lace-ups *de rigueur*—pinstripe suits are made to be worn with
the proper footwear. Rei Kawakubo of Comme des Garçons
rarely uses a heel. Her brightly colored cowboy shoes
of fall/winter 1999–2000 were a great hit with the
fashion crowd because they were flat shoes designed
to be noticed. In the 1980s shoes by Doc Martens and

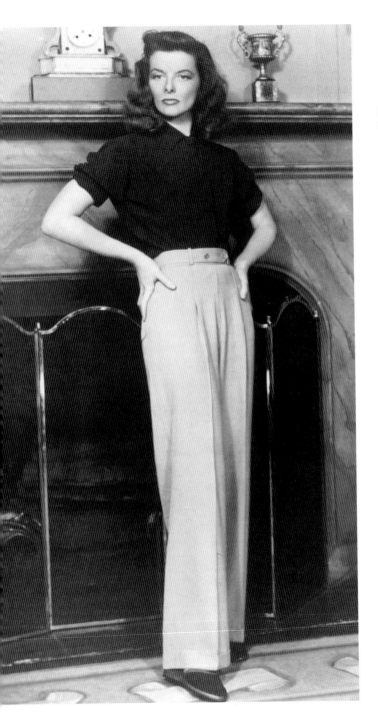

KATHARINE HEPBURN ALWAYS LOOKED CHIC IN A MAN'S SHIRT, WIDE SLACKS, AND MASCULINE SHOES

loafers by Gucci were as fashionable as killer stilettos and shoulder pads. In the 1970s there was the dreaded rope sandal, and in the 1960s a long, flat pointed-toe style was the hit of the decade. And, of course, there is always the classic masculine Katharine Hepburn look—wide flannel slacks accented with men's oxfords.

Many American sportswear companies favor flats because they are functional and modern. Donna Karan believes in comfort as well as style; her Fifth Avenue woman wears flat shoes to travel to work, but might change into a heel when she gets there. The flattest of shoes have to be slippers. Since the late 1990s, there has been a trend for wearing slippers outside of the home. Of course, these are not ordinary standard carpet slippers. They come in the form of elaborately embroidered and sequined silk slip-ons from the East. Some designers, including Paul Smith, have included

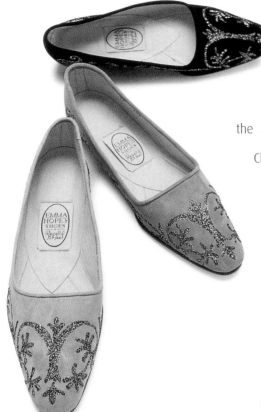

them in their collections, and even Marks & Spencer sells them. They followed in the footsteps of the Chinese cheongsam "Suzy Wong" dress and have made Chinatowns from New York to London a prime hunting ground for shoe hounds. Of course, a single pair will not do. Any shoe that costs so little must be bought in bulk—with a pair in every color for every conceivable outfit.

SLIPPERS HAVE METAMORPHOSED INTO OUTDOOR SHOES, EVERY BIT AS FRIVOLOUS AS EMBROIDERED HEELS, ABOVE. RIGHT, CAMPER ADDS A BIT OF WIT AND HUMOR TO A PAIR OF FLATTIES. THE MISMATCHED SHOES ARE CALLED "TWINS"

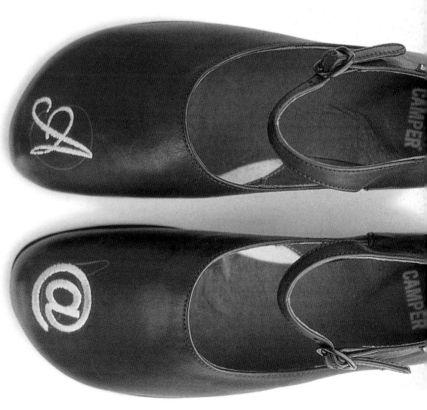

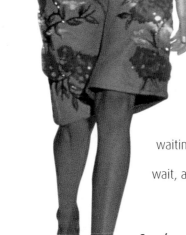

waiting lists

If you have ever joined a waiting list for a pair of shoes, you can safely be classified as a Grade A shoeaholic. You need help. The problem with seeing a shoe on the catwalk, or in a photograph in the next day's newspaper, is that it can take up to six months before the desired objects are on sale. And if, after your long and arduous wait, you do not get to the store on the day of the delivery, you run the risk of the only two pairs in your size being sold out.

Some companies limit production of a particular shoe (often a shoe that will feature in their advertising) so that demand 'way outstrips supply. The result? Near hysteria when stocks run out. Take Gucci's hand-beaded kitten-heel slingbacks from spring/summer 2000. One fashion editor eagerly put her name on the waiting list, but she could not wait, and on a trip to Milan

GUCCI'S BEADED SLINGBACKS WERE WORTH THE WAIT, WHILE THE COMPANY'S LOAFER IS STILL A CLASSIC

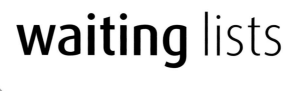

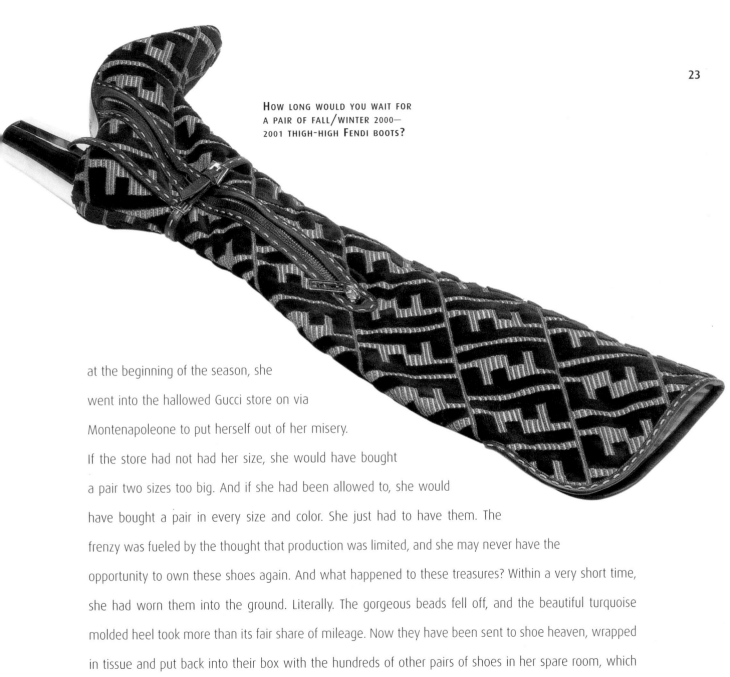

HOW LONG WOULD YOU WAIT FOR
A PAIR OF FALL/WINTER 2000—
2001 THIGH-HIGH **FENDI** BOOTS?

at the beginning of the season, she

went into the hallowed Gucci store on via

Montenapoleone to put herself out of her misery.

If the store had not had her size, she would have bought

a pair two sizes too big. And if she had been allowed to, she would

have bought a pair in every size and color. She just had to have them. The

frenzy was fueled by the thought that production was limited, and she may never have the

opportunity to own these shoes again. And what happened to these treasures? Within a very short time,

she had worn them into the ground. Literally. The gorgeous beads fell off, and the beautiful turquoise

molded heel took more than its fair share of mileage. Now they have been sent to shoe heaven, wrapped

in tissue and put back into their box with the hundreds of other pairs of shoes in her spare room, which doubles as a shoe graveyard. It is quite possible that they will never see the light of day again.

The great thing about shoes is that there is always a new style just around the corner—with a brand-new heel or an elegant bit of beading to drool over. And, of course, there is always another waiting list to join. Hot on the beaded straps of the Fendi baguette bag is the brand's "double F" heeled shoe. Before the shoe had even made its way off the runway for the Italian luxury goods house's fall/winter 2000—2001 collection, the fashion pack had put it into their mental shopping baskets.

At Prada, you are guaranteed to find a waiting list for a particular shoe size or style. For fall/winter 1998—1999, it was the leather foliage appliqué shoe that attracted the frenzy—partly because it was a trademark Prada shoe and partly because it was used in the company's advertising. For spring/summer 2000, it was the kitten heel with photo-print lips and hearts, as well as the crocodile heels in pink, red, and purple,

PRADA'S THORNY LEAF DESIGN WAS A SIGNATURE OF THE SEASON. TO SECURE THE SHOE, DEDICATED FASHIONISTAS PUT THEIR NAMES ON THE WAITING LIST UP TO A SEASON AHEAD

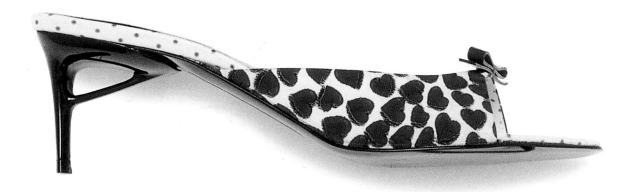

with handbags to match. Once a customer had bought one, it was hard to resist the other. And for winter 2000—2001, the list of buyers was already growing six months before the label's black leather boot was launched. It's a guaranteed sellout, whatever the style. Who knows what styles of footwear people will be waiting for in 2010?

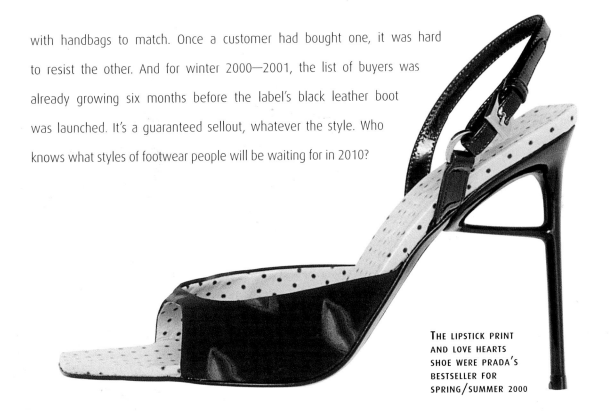

THE LIPSTICK PRINT AND LOVE HEARTS SHOE WERE PRADA'S BESTSELLER FOR SPRING/SUMMER 2000

precious moments

When Antonio Berardi transported the shoes for his spring/summer 1999 collection to the London venue, they traveled with their own personal bodyguard. The previous season, Berardi's collection had been stolen on the street outside his studio, but that was not the only reason. Twelve of the shoe boxes were worth their weight in gold. Literally. These were not so much shoes as jewels, complete with gold chains and straps made from finest 18-carat gold. Backstage at the show they were never let out of sight, counted onto the models' feet and off again. Each pair was worth $12,000.

The gold shoe idea is typical of Berardi. They were made by the master shoemaker Manolo Blahnik, who was also responsible for the wooden clogs decorated with hand-blown Murano glass leaves and flowers from Berardi's spring/summer 1998 collection. But the gold shoes were claimed to be the most expensive shoes ever made. Of course, there are several other claims for this feat, and Gina, the London shoe company, has managed to get its most precious shoes into the *Guinness Book of Records*—a pair of $25,000, hand-crafted alligator mules, finished with white-gold buckles inlaid with 36 Princess-cut diamonds. They claim to have sold a few pairs, too.

FERRAGAMO'S
18-CARAT GOLD SHOE
WITH CARVED HEELS
SET THE TONE FOR
SHOES THAT DOUBLE
AS PRECIOUS JEWELS

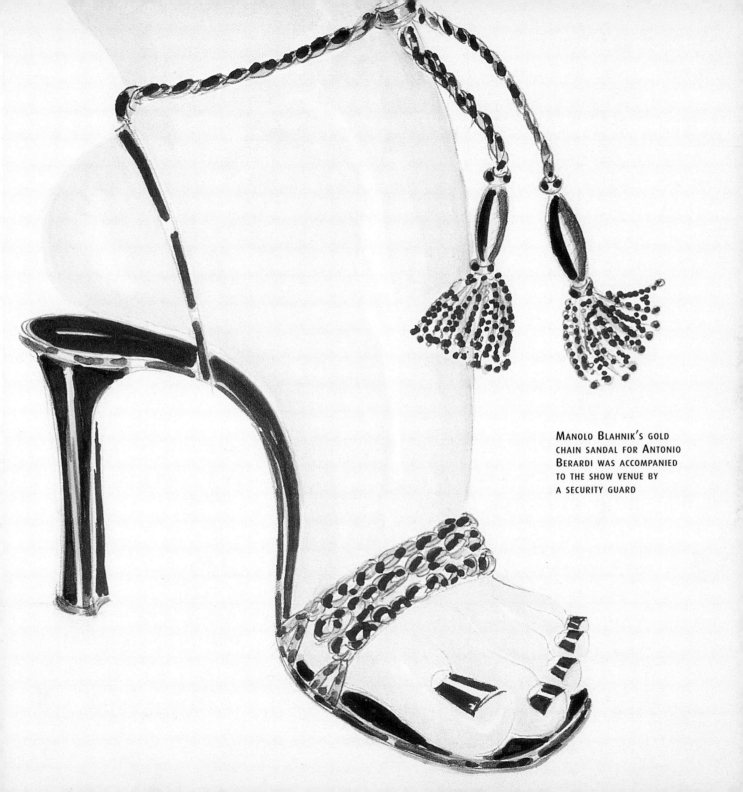

MANOLO BLAHNIK'S GOLD
CHAIN SANDAL FOR ANTONIO
BERARDI WAS ACCOMPANIED
TO THE SHOW VENUE BY
A SECURITY GUARD

GINA'S DIAMOND-STUDDED
BUCKLES, RIGHT. MARILYN'S
RUBY RHINESTONE-ENCRUSTED
SHOES, OPPOSITE, DESIGNED
BY FERRAGAMO, WERE SOLD
AT AUCTION IN 1999 FOR
A RECORD $48,300

The idea of shoes as jewelery is not new. In September 1999 a pair of ruby rhinestone-encrusted shoes was sold at Christie's in London for $48,300. The estimate was $4,000–$6,000. The shoes were once the property of Marilyn Monroe and were made for her by Salvatore Ferragamo. Not a fraction of an inch of the red satin shoes was left uncovered by rhinestones, which twinkled in every direction. How could anyone have resisted looking at such precious objects? Especially when they were on the feet of the luscious Ms. Monroe. The shoes were bought back by the Ferragamo family, who have since put a reproduction into their collection. But it was not just movie stars who wanted their shoes to be accompanied by a jewelery box and padlock. In 1956 Ferragamo made a pair of 18-carat gold sandals for an Australian client. They cost $1,000—at that price, perhaps the greatest indulgence a woman could have. But with their intricately carved three-and-a-half-inch heels and heavy twisted gold chains at the ankle and across the foot, attached to the sole with tiny bells, the shoes were worth every cent. The sandal is now on display at the Ferragamo collection in Palazzo Feroni. Salvatore Ferragamo also made shoes for Eva Perón. She preferred animal skins to gold and jewels, the rarer the better.

There is something quite contradictory about wearing a pair of precious shoes. They are, after all, designed to protect the feet from coming into contact with the ground. To wear a pair of shoes worth $12,000 apiece, you risk being mugged and having your shoes unceremoniously removed at knife point. Such shoes are for teetering from limo to theater, or from ballroom to limo. The gold Ferragamo sandals look as though they were worn about three times. But then, Marlene Dietrich, another

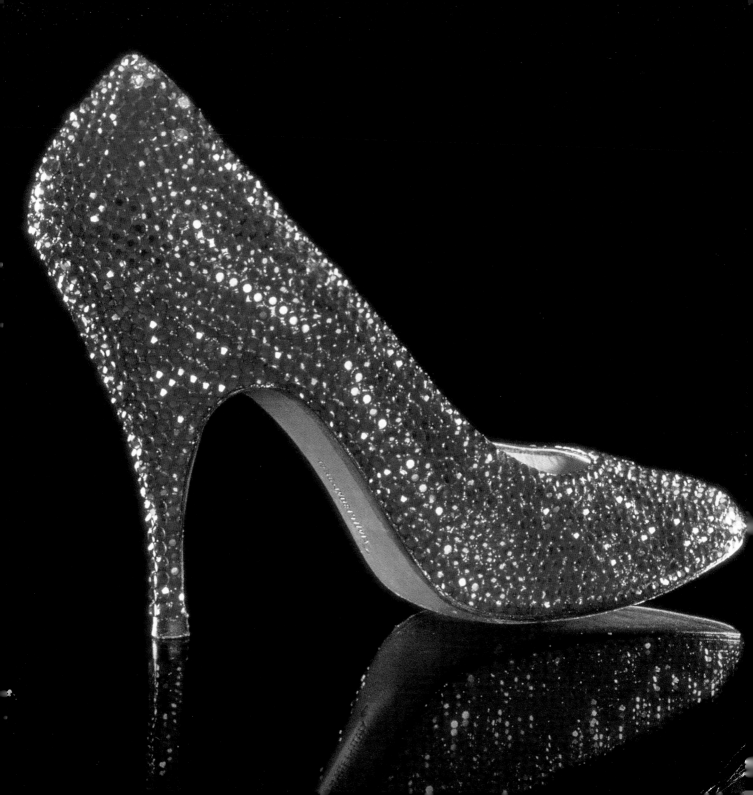

Ferragamo customer, never wore her shoes more than twice. With shoes this precious, you would simply want to put them on a pedestal and worship them.

Expensive shoes are a supreme indulgence, but Ferragamo is not the only designer to take them to the height of decadence. Manolo Blahnik has a long-standing collaboration with John Galliano, whose own romantic vision is one that translates perfectly into shoes. Between them, they have produced some of the most fantastic and elaborate shoes imaginable. There have been high-heeled, strappy shoe-boots inspired by Masai warriors, all beads and mother-of-pearl buttons. There have been showgirl boots, beaded and sequined to tell the story of a collection all on their own. Most recently, the two men have conspired to make some of the most wickedly decadent shoes for the house of Christian Dior: one collection featured platform mules finished with mink, while for fall/winter 2000—2001, there are elegant heels echoing those designed by Roger Vivier for Dior

MANOLO BLAHNIK USED FEATHERS INTRICATELY SEWN TOGETHER FOR THIS SLIPPER, ABOVE. RHINESTONE-ENCRUSTED SOLES FOR DIOR'S FALL/WINTER 2000—2001 SHOWN OFF ON A MIRRORED CATWALK, OPPOSITE

in 1956. The best way to see the design of the shoes from all angles is on a mirror, and for Dior's haute-couture spring/summer 2000 show, Galliano presented them on a mirrored catwalk. The backs of the heels are encrusted with glittering rhinestones and—here is the really glamorous bit—the soles are diamond-studded, too, an idea that both Halston and Valentino also explored.

Rhinestone-studded shoes need a special occasion to be shown off (although just wearing them around the house is quite an event in itself). What greater occasion is there than a coronation? When

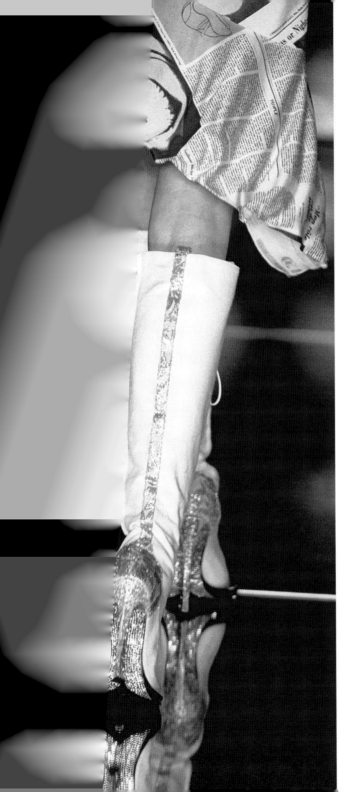

Queen Elizabeth II was crowned in 1953, her shoes
were made by the French designer Roger Vivier. They
were made of gold kidskin and studded with garnets
that flashed like rubies, a symbol of her marriage to
her country. One French magazine recognized the fine
art of Roger Vivier heels in 1962 when it commented:
"Roger Vivier's evening shoes are the works of a
jeweler rather than a shoemaker. Only empresses and
queens of the screen can indulge in them."

For many women, however, their most precious
shoe moment comes on their wedding day. The
famous have particular scope to indulge in such a
special-occasion shoe. Sophie Rhys Jones was married
in hand-sewn Gina shoes, and Posh Spice was married
in a silver pair, designed exclusively for her by Mr.
Blahnik himself. Ironically, wedding shoes—often the
most expensive pair of shoes a woman will own—are
usually only worn once. They are designed to be as
close to Cinderella's glass slippers as possible. These
shoes are most certainly not made for walking. Sipping
champagne from them is optional.

clump clump

What is it about rebellious teenagers, fashion victims, and ugly shoes? There seems to be some strange magnetic attraction. The uglier a shoe, the more likely it is to be a bestseller, even if only for a season. Frankenstein is a big influence on shoe design, as are orthopedic shoes. The late fashion icon, artist's muse, and nightclub host, Leigh Bowery, understood the relationship. His bizarre footwear—one high-rise club foot and one lower platform, worn under a pair of tights—could have been more influential than even he thought possible. The avant-garde French shoe designer Benoit Méleard, whose bright ideas have included the strap-on heel worn in place of a shoe, and the American designer Jeremy Scott, who creates shoes with mismatched heel heights, draw inspiration from Bowery. And you need only look at a gang of

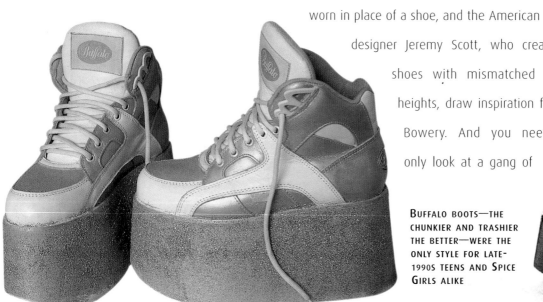

BUFFALO BOOTS—THE CHUNKIER AND TRASHIER THE BETTER—WERE THE ONLY STYLE FOR LATE-1990S TEENS AND SPICE GIRLS ALIKE

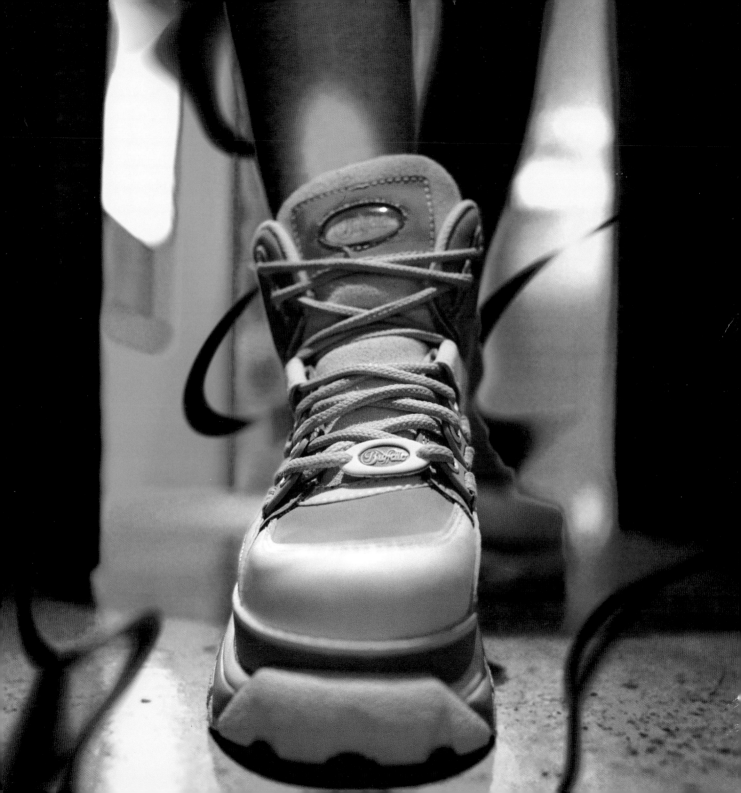

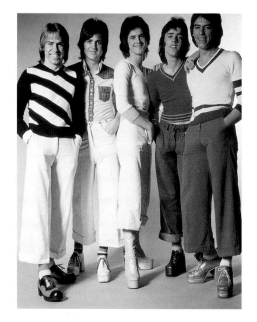

teenagers hanging out on a Saturday afternoon, in Tokyo, Milan, or SoHo, to see the influence: great hulking trainers mounted on platforms of rubber that reach up to eight inches in height.

At the height of the Frankenstein shoe craze in the late 1990s, Buffalo was the brand to be seen in. The Spice Girls wore them, and they became cult items, to be updated almost weekly. There were glitter boots in candy colors, trainers, slip-ons, and soles that kept on rising. Even Christian Lacroix joined in the fun in 1996 with his metallic pink and gold trainers on stripy multicolored platforms.

The great decade of shoe horrors, however, remains the 1970s, when Gary Glitter, the Bay City Rollers, and Elton John all took footwear into another dimension. Nothing was too vulgar, too high, too shiny, or too sparkly. Terry de Havilland, the London-based shoe designer, made platforms by stitching patches of brightly colored leather together to give a handmade, homespun look. If the 1970s superfly clothes made the wearer look as though she was about to flap her shirt collars and take off, the platforms kept her feet on the ground like lead weights.

The other 1970s shoe favorite that enjoyed a revival in the late 1990s was the Cornish Pasty. Hush Puppies specialized in

1970S HEELS AND PLATFORMS WERE BIG AND CLUNKY

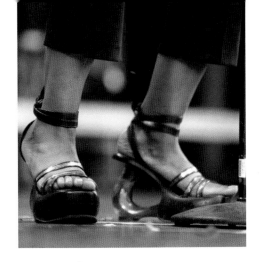

KELE LE ROC'S LOOPY WEDGES

making spoon-shaped leather shoes that did nothing to disguise thick, exposed seams and extra-wide shoe fittings. They gave new meaning to the Cockney rhyming slang phrase "plates of meat" for "feet." In the late 1990s the Cornish Pasty enjoyed cult status, with the seamed desert trek boot being worn by Robbie Williams and Oasis. They were so ugly, they were cool. The same could be said of Birkenstock clogs and sandals, which have spawned many a chain-store rip-off. They are anything but sleek and sharp, but fashion groupies love them.

DOLCE E GABBANA, RIGHT. GERMAN COMPANY TRIPPEN'S Y2K WOODEN CLOGS, BELOW, HARK BACK TO TRADITIONAL FOOTWEAR

Germany has a reputation for producing a certain kind of shoe that is good for the feet and the environment, and just the thing to form a cult following. Trippen is a small company set up by two designers, Angela Spieth and Michael Oehler, in 1992. They wanted to make shoes that mixed high fashion and ecology consciousness, and came up with a wood-and-leather clog. Joop, Yohji Yamamoto, and Perry Ellis have used them on the catwalk. More recently, they developed the sole into a gentle wave that mimics the form of the foot.

shoes & **status**

Some shoes are little more than an advertising tool. They work on two levels: they have so many logos and signatures on them, they are the equivalent of holding a branded shopping bag. Wherever you walk, they advertise. Customers should, in fact, be paid to wear them. Such shoes function on another level; they announce the fact that the wearer is wealthy (even if the purchase means that he or she is left eating baked beans for the rest of the month), shrieking money and status from their very soles.

Although the 1980s were regarded as the main era of status dressing, the twenty-first century is gearing up for some serious competition. The collections in early 2000 marked the beginning of logo mania, be it a Louis Vuitton bag or Christian Dior denim boots with repeat CD logos interlocking from ankle to knee. Céline, the French

ADIDAS, HERMÈS, AND CHANEL ALL HAVE THEIR OWN SIGNATURES, WHICH SEND OUT SIGNALS TO THOSE IN THE KNOW

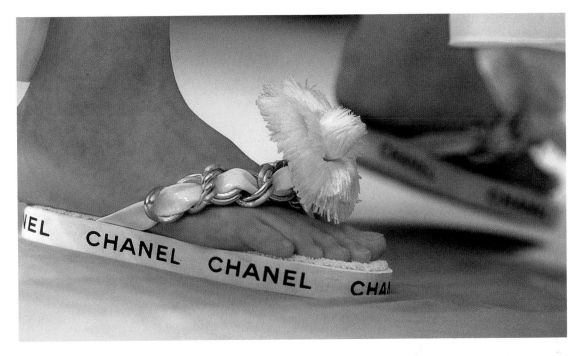

luxury leather house, scattered its logo over high heels, and the Italian house Fendi has spread the F-word via its trainers. Even the discreetly low-key French company Hermès has Hs stitched into its $300 sneakers.

The obsession with brand names started in the 1980s when the cult of the designer really exploded. Depending on your preferences for music and fashion, brands meant different things to different people. Three Adidas stripes might have been the coolest logo to wear on your feet for Run DMC and their fans, while the Gucci loafer (and it had to be the real thing) and an upturned collar were all the Sloane Ranger needed to be part of the gang. Put simply, branding is about identifying with a particular style tribe: if you wanted to show that you were wealthy and in the know, a pair of simple two-tone pumps by Chanel would do the trick. There did not even have to be a pair of Cs in sight—if you were part of the gang, or aspired to be part of the gang, those pumps said it all.

The difference between the logo excess of the 1980s and that of the twenty-first century is that, apparently, logo mania is now all about irony. When the hip London designer Luella Bartley wears her

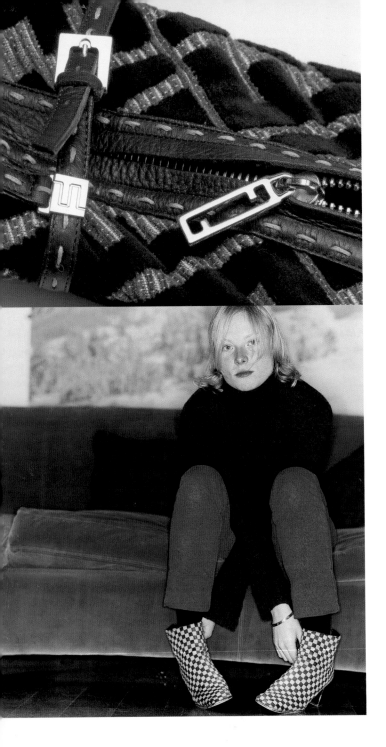

Damier check boots by Louis Vuitton, she wears them with a pair of jeans and an air of utter indifference. She is not so much showing off her status in life as saying, "Yeah, I'm wearing Louis Vuitton boots. So what?"

The new branding excesses are all done with tongue firmly in cheek. Or are they? When Li'l Kim wears a pair of Dior denim boots (which were designed by John Galliano with rap stars like her in mind), she is proud of the wealth and the lifestyle they represent, just as the Knightsbridge brat blatantly flaunted her Chanel heels 20 years previously. There is something particularly fabulous, even "ghetto fabulous," about mixing denim, that most workaday of fabrics, with the glitzy gold initials of a luxury goods company.

As well as linking Cs, gold CDs, Nike flashes, and Adidas stripes, perhaps one of the most potent logos is a single discreet red stripe—all it takes to identify a pair of Prada Sport shoes from 50 paces, and a surefire indication of somebody

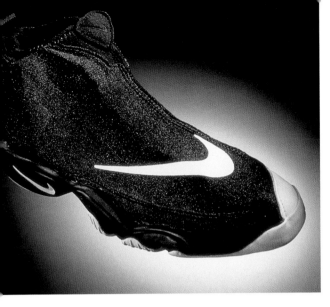

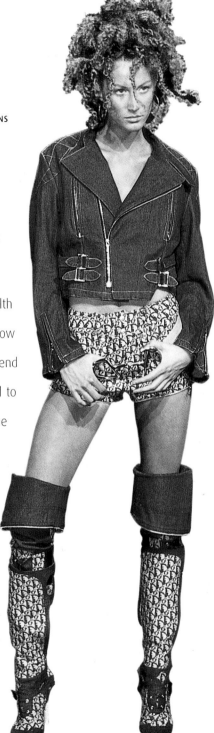

FENDI USES THE INITIAL F
EVERYWHERE, EVEN ON ITS
ZIPPERS, OPPOSITE TOP.
LONDON DESIGNER LUELLA
BARTLEY, OPPOSITE BOTTOM,
WEARS LOUIS VUITTON BOOTS
WITH A PAIR OF HER OWN JEANS

THE NIKE FLASH, LEFT,
GIVES THE WEARER
A POSITIVE FEELING

JOHN GALLIANO'S SPRING/
SUMMER 2000 COLLECTION
FOR DIOR MAKES FULL USE
OF THE HOUSE'S LOGO TO GIVE
THESE DENIM BOOTS, RIGHT,
MAXIMUM ATTITUDE

really in the know. You could never be accused of flaunting your wealth with such a simple graphic device. Nevertheless, the Prada stripe tells fellow fashionistas that the wearer is serious about her shoes and willing to spend large chunks of cash to prove it. However, she is a very different animal to the woman who likes to flaunt her designer logos outrageously on all she wears. She does not scream her allegiance to Prada, she whispers it.

With or without irony, the logo trend promises to continue well into the twenty-first century if its early years are anything to go by. The fall/winter 2000—2001 collection by Karl Lagerfeld for Fendi shrieks designer excess, from the handbags and manicured nails to the flash of metal on the steel heels made from two interlocking Fs. Even the zipper echoes the design, a subliminal message that will not let you, or anyone else, forget what label you are wearing. After all, if a woman is to wear a multicolored fur coat, she needs to dress her feet up a little.

kinky boots

40

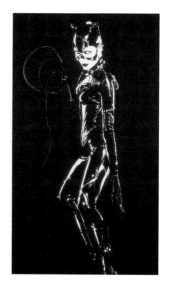

CATWOMAN'S THIGH-HIGH
BOOTS, ABOVE, ARE ALL
PART OF HER FELINE APPEAL.
THE CLASSIC KINKY BOOT,
RIGHT, IS BLACK, SHINY,
AND VERY, VERY HIGH

In fifteenth-century Venice, prostitutes wore ridiculously high platform heels—virtually stilts—so that they would stand tall from the crowd and be noticed. Such shoes would have looked ridiculous on the ordinary woman, but for the prostitute they added a frisson of danger and debauchery. Traditionally, the shoes of a prostitute have marked their profession: high, shiny, and very, very pointed, they parody the femininity of a high heel. When transvestites wear high heels, they also like to take them to the max. Like a woman who has a breast enlargement, what is the point of going up one cup size when you can go up three?

Take a look in the store windows of a red-light district in any city in the world, and you will see a range of heels so dangerously high that you can safely conclude they are not designed for walking. Although the very opposite of carpet slippers, they are meant to be worn in the bedroom. So, too, are "kinky" boots. So what makes them kinky? Their length, usually to the thigh; the shininess of the leather— usually scarlet or black; the laces that tie naughtily up the leg; and, of course, the height of the heel.

As with all forms of extreme dress, the kinky boot has been embraced by the fashion industry and female superheroes alike. Catwoman, who was always something of a male fantasy, wore them. So, too, did Diana Rigg's Emma Peel (or M-Appeal for man appeal) in the 1960s television series *The Avengers*. But the buckles and bondage of the sex industry have been a favorite theme with fashion designers, too. The French designer Thierry Mugler makes no pretence about his inspiration, frequently using leather, rubber, bondage corsetry, and kinky boots galore—clothes for drag queens or S&M fashion queens.

The late Gianni Versace's collections were always designed to be worn with high-heeled shoes or boots, with more than a hint of the S&M dominatrix. His entire collection for fall/winter 1992—1993 revolved around the theme of gladiators and bondage. Needless to say, the boots were high and buckled up the leg to above the knee, each buckle fastening with a signature Medusa's head in gold. His highly jeweled and decorated shoes always fetishized the female foot. Gianni's younger sister Donatella, who has taken over the creative control

WHAT COULD BE NAUGHTIER THAN JANE FONDA WITH HER THIGH BOOTS AND GUN?

of the company, was seemingly born and bred in the highest of heels, and she continues the tradition of highly sexed shoes in her collections.

Fellow Italians—Sergio Rossi, Gucci, and Dolce e Gabbana (whose heels have featured padlocks and chains)—have all produced shoes with an indecent amount of warped sex appeal, though it is the British designer Vivienne Westwood who has blurred the lines between sex and fashion most effectively. Throughout her career, Westwood has fetishized her clothes. The 1974 Malcolm McLaren and Vivienne Westwood store was, after all, simply called SEX. It is an obsession that has been a constant theme in her collections since the days of punk. Along with bondage trousers, there were peephole pants and the masturbation skirt, as well as a serious amount of shoe fetishization. Her famous elevator platforms hark back to the fifteenth-century Venetian chopine, while her black patent-leather "penis shoe" of the 1980s made the wearer's foot a walking dildo. Typically, Westwood has subverted the idea of the sexy shoe into something sinister and threatening. While a strappy, bright red Sergio Rossi might make a woman look seductively saucy, a Westwood shoe brings out the darker side of S&M: the woman who wears these heels is no submissive sex kitten.

MANOLO BLAHNIK'S BOOTS, RIGHT, SAUCILY LACE UP THE BACK. DOLCE E GABBANA'S STRICT BOOTS, OPPOSITE LEFT. VERSACE CAN ALWAYS BE RELIED UPON TO PUT A LITTLE FRISSON INTO ITS FOOTWEAR, OPPOSITE RIGHT

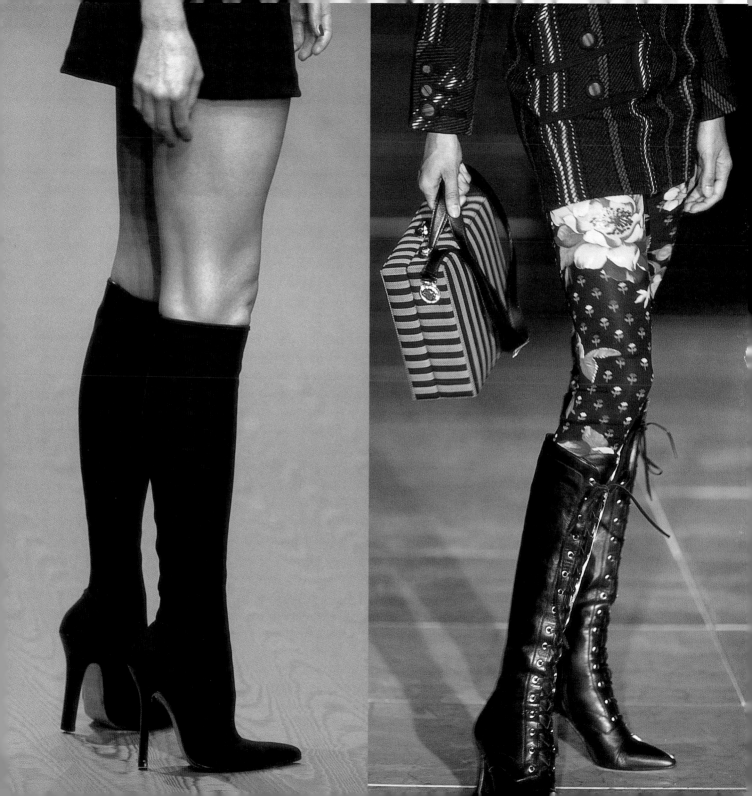

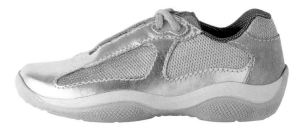

Prada's Sport line sums it up: a fashion collection that takes high-performance sports and the most advanced, up-to-the-minute technology as seriously as it takes styling and design. The two feed off each other. Since sportswear and trainer brands have become as desirable as fashion labels, sport and technology have been intertwined. Both sports and fashion brands are striving for the same thing: shoes that are at the cutting edge of design and technology.

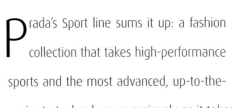

The average Nike trainer is made up of 34 different components. It is no longer enough that a sports shoe fits the wearer and is bouncy. It must also offer protection against injury, as well as giving the player enhanced performance potential. A trainer does not begin life on a designer's drawing board, but with a team of biomechanics in the research lab. Every shoe is under constant revision to find

techno

out how its performance can be improved. Since 1979, when the Nike Tailwind shoe was launched, which featured the first Nike-Air gas cushioning in the sole, there have been numerous improvements to the Nike-Air technology. Over the years, researchers have developed new ways of adding cushioning to the shoe and more air into the sole. By 1996, with the Max Air, Nike had a shoe whose specifications read more like those of an airplane than a shoe. By that point, the Air-Sole units, which offered visibility to the gas inside, were as much a feature to show off on the dance floor as on the sports field. Suddenly, it was hip to be a trainer geek, and to know your Monkey Paw (a protection device used in basketball footwear) from your Goat Traction (Nike's unique "dual-density rubber outsole engineered for supreme traction and stability").

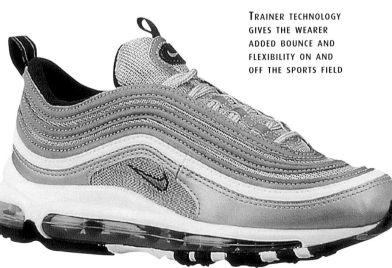

TRAINER TECHNOLOGY GIVES THE WEARER ADDED BOUNCE AND FLEXIBILITY ON AND OFF THE SPORTS FIELD

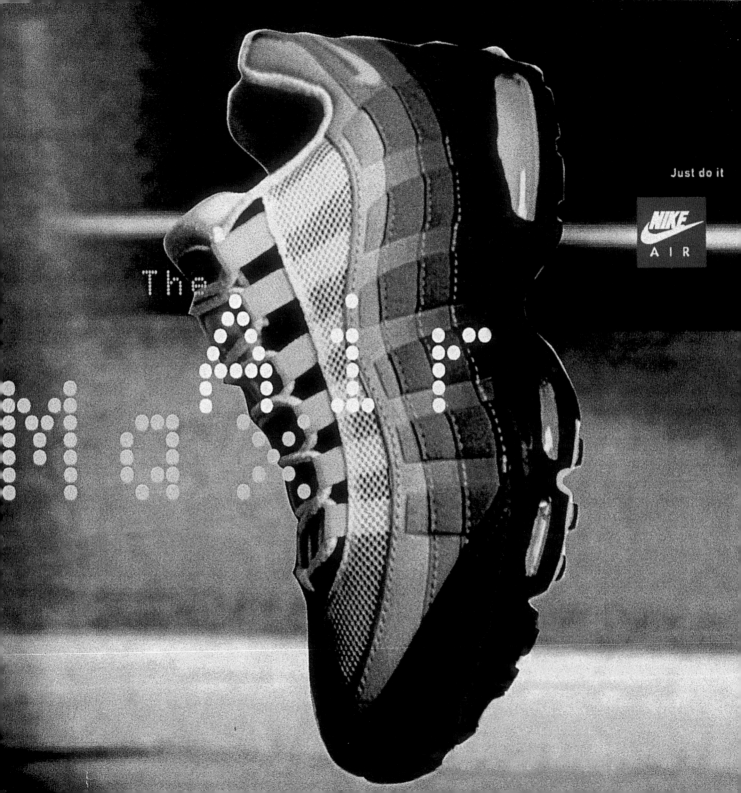

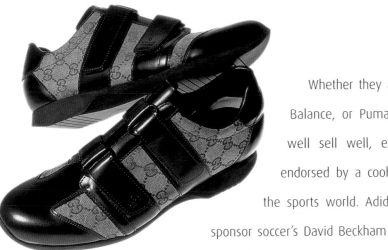

NIKE AIR MAX, OPPOSITE, ARE BUILT FOR PERFORMANCE. GUCCI AND PRADA TRAINERS, LEFT AND BELOW, ARE FOR THOSE WITH A PRIVATE GYM

Whether they are Adidas, Nike, New Balance, or Puma, shoes that perform well sell well, especially if they are endorsed by a cool figure from the sports world. Adidas sponsor soccer's David Beckham to wear his three stripes, and Michael Jordan has his own shoe named after him. In the late 1990s people who did not so much as jog to work in the morning began to buy trainers as their casual shoes. Serious obsessives even took to buying two pairs at once—one to wear and the other to keep shrink-wrapped as a collector's item for the future. The Nike Air Rift, with its split toe, is a classic example of a shoe guaranteed to attract the attention of the serious trainer spotter. It is named after the Rift Valley in Kenya, and, apparently, the split toe is designed to give runners a powerful push-off. Quite why a trainer fiend like Antonio Berardi needs better performance for "pushing off" on a run is a mystery. But he—and, it has to be said, trainer fanatics are mostly men—wears them all the same.

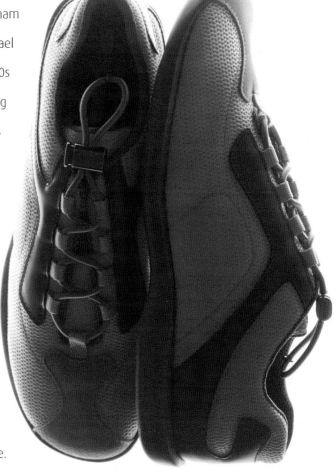

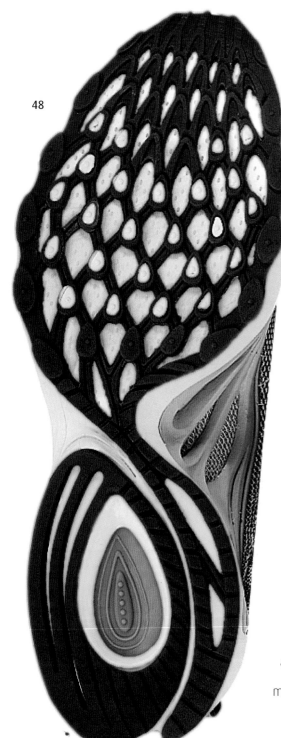

It is no wonder that fashion labels wanted a piece of the action. Fendi, Gucci, Donna Karan, Chanel, and Hermès have all included trainers as part of their collections. The price tags on some of these shoes make the real thing look like bargain-basement buys. But then, these shoes are about status. No one seriously expects a woman to go spinning or jogging in her quilted Chanel trainers, unless, that is, she happens to be in a gym at some chichi hotel in Capri. Prada and Ralph Lauren have gone one step farther. They wanted their sports gear to be taken seriously, so they introduced their own Sport labels. Their commitment has paid off; some of their more basic, less fashion-oriented shoes would not look out of place in the more well-heeled gyms. There are also brands that specialize in making trainers for fashion. The Australian company Royal Elastics is a prime example. The designers get their inspiration from nightclub dance floors rather than the minutiae of a basketball player's foot movements. Shoes from the British company Acupuncture are more about attitude—punk rebellion—and style than performance.

The trainer industry has begun to parody itself. It is no longer a symbol of all that is hip and cutting edge, but all that is utterly mainstream. The trainer has become as universal as denim jeans. What is interesting, however, is how advanced technology is being applied to everyday footwear, making a new hybrid of shoes that combine function and fashion. Prada has taken the elements of the trainer—the fabric, the lacing system, and the injection-molded sole—and made them into high heels. These shoes might be slightly more practical for trotting to catch a bus in than the average pair of spike heels, but running a race in them is not advisable. Hi-tech fabrics like Gore-Tex, Velcro, and Neoprene, as well as technological advances in manufacturing, have all played a part in shaping a new generation of footwear.

The relationship works both ways. The Nike Air Moc—an easy, slip-on moccasin that is aerodynamic and features a drawstring and sporty toggle—is the closest sportswear has come to the carpet slipper. So, too, the Aqua sock, made into sharp, urban wear by Donna Karan, who produced her own version. These funny, organic, molded-to-the-foot shoes are perfect for lounging on a Sunday afternoon, even though they are designed with light hiking and water sports in mind.

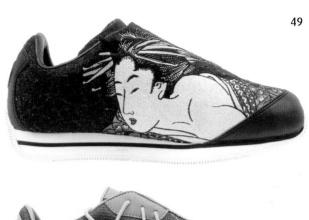

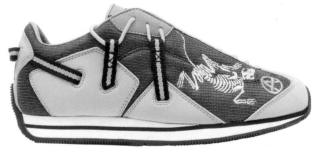

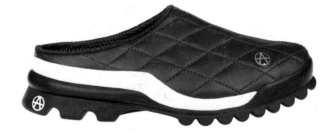

ACUPUNCTURE'S STREETWISE TRAINERS, ABOVE, ARE MORE ABOUT STYLING AND FASHION THAN FUNCTION. THE TRAINER SPECIFICATIONS FOR A NIKE SOLE, OPPOSITE, ARE ENOUGH TO MAKE TRAINER GEEKS UPDATE THEIR SHOES EVERY SIX WEEKS

21st-century shoes

If the turn of the nineteenth century was the beginning of the designer shoe, the turn of the twentieth century could mark the advent of the do-it-yourself shoe. In fashion, there is a trend toward customization and individuality; perhaps it is a reaction against the parallel trend toward labels and logos. But this is not the customization of the punk days, when clothes were distressed, written on, and safety-pinned by their owners. The customization of the twenty-first century is altogether slicker. Levi wearers can now design their own jeans by using an in-store computer program that allows them to have their name embroidered on a pocket, or to choose the finish of the denim. Websites, too, like the Norwegian cybercouture.com, allow shoppers to have an

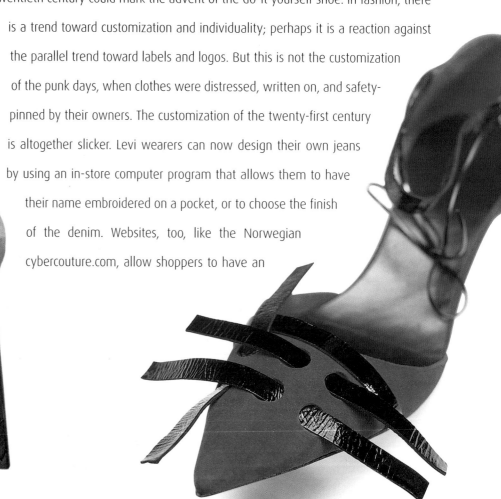

outfit custom-made to fit their own measurements. And Nike.com has launched Nike iD, a section of its website that allows customers to design their own trainers. Customers in the U.S. are given a choice of four different styles and can choose the color, the sole, the color of the Nike flash, and even give their trainer their own eight-letter ID. This is only the start of a whole new generation of shoe and fashion design that allows the customer to virtually design their own clothes, while offering big corporations the chance to give their customers a service previously only available at small, made-to-order companies.

The young Danish innovator As Øland graduated from London's Royal College of Art in the summer of 2000. She specialized in footwear, but not in the traditional way. Her shoes come in kit form, to be made as the wearer desires. You simply collect different components and click them together in whichever configuration you like. A shoe can be changed according to the weather. "The whole fashion today is about individuality," she says. "You can put your personality into your shoes."

AS ØLAND'S INGENIOUS SHOES, OPPOSITE, COME IN KIT FORM, TO CUSTOMIZE AS THE WEARER LIKES. PATRICK COX HAS ALSO MADE A KIT SHOE, RIGHT, WITH CLIP-ON PARTS FOR HIS FALL/WINTER 2000—2001 COLLECTION

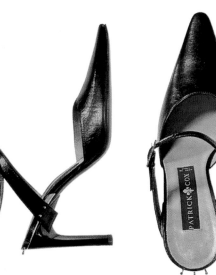
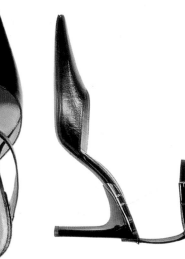

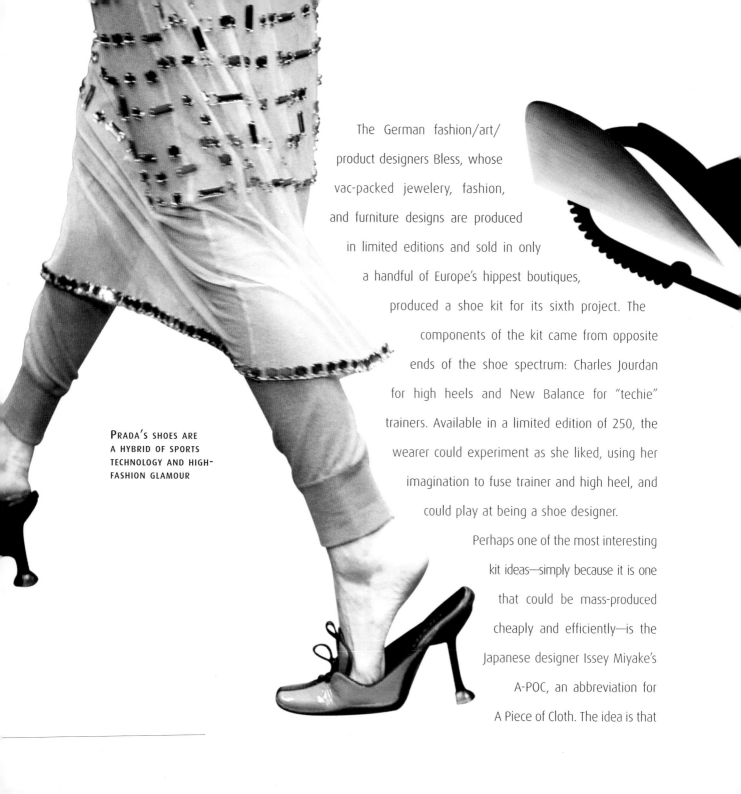

The German fashion/art/ product designers Bless, whose vac-packed jewelery, fashion, and furniture designs are produced in limited editions and sold in only a handful of Europe's hippest boutiques, produced a shoe kit for its sixth project. The components of the kit came from opposite ends of the shoe spectrum: Charles Jourdan for high heels and New Balance for "techie" trainers. Available in a limited edition of 250, the wearer could experiment as she liked, using her imagination to fuse trainer and high heel, and could play at being a shoe designer.

Perhaps one of the most interesting kit ideas—simply because it is one that could be mass-produced cheaply and efficiently—is the Japanese designer Issey Miyake's A-POC, an abbreviation for A Piece of Cloth. The idea is that

PRADA'S SHOES ARE A HYBRID OF SPORTS TECHNOLOGY AND HIGH-FASHION GLAMOUR

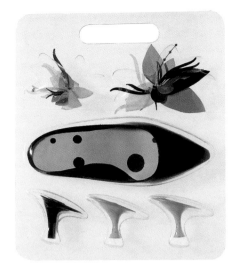

an entire outfit can be cut from a single ingeniously knitted and perforated cloth. In addition to a dress, panties, bra top, bag, and socks, the A-POC collection features a futuristic vision of shoes.

While conventional shoes using leather, suede, reptile skins, and synthetics will exist as long as there are feet to put in them, there is a move toward ecology and sustainability in shoe design. German companies Birkenstock, with its cork soles, and Trippen, with its use of renewable wood, are leading the way. So, too, is Camper, the Majorcan company, which has made its name with its traditional country shoe made from recycled tires, canvas, and string. One of Camper's most forward-looking shoes is the ACS, or Active Compact Shoe, which uses new technology to make a shoe that is light, aerodynamic, and, best of all, washable. They are the perfect combination of technology and good sense.

TRIPPEN'S WOOD-AND-LEATHER SANDALS, ABOVE, LOOK POSITIVELY SCI-FI. AS ØLAND'S KIT-SHOE PACK, TOP

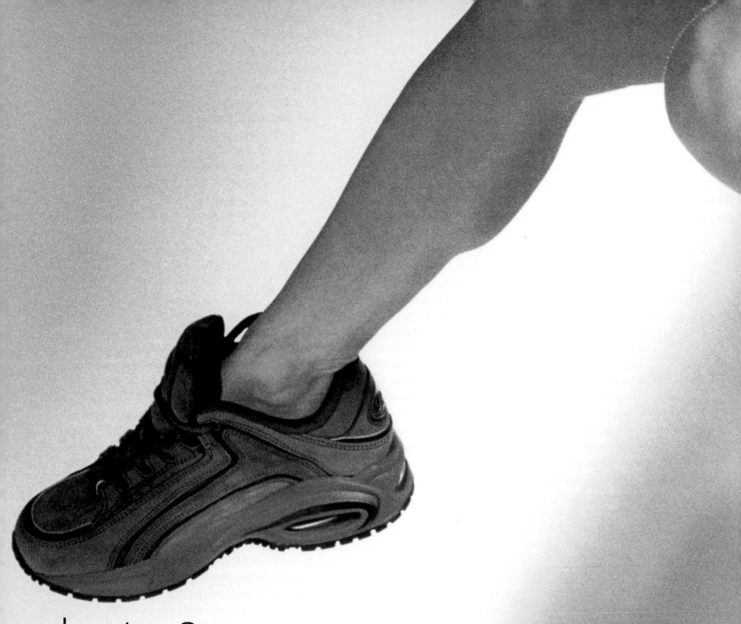

chapter 2

THE **WHO'S WHO** OF SHOES

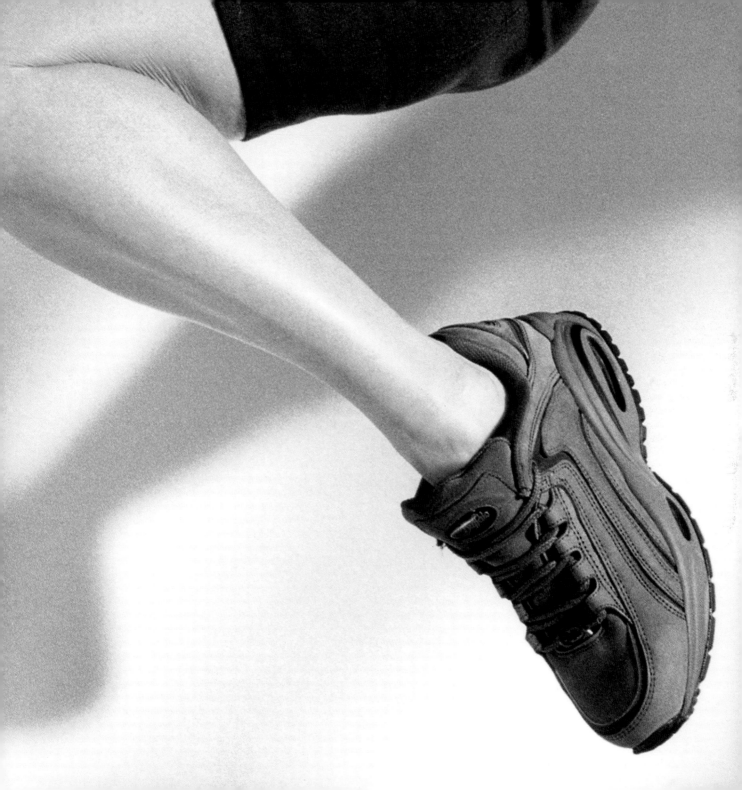

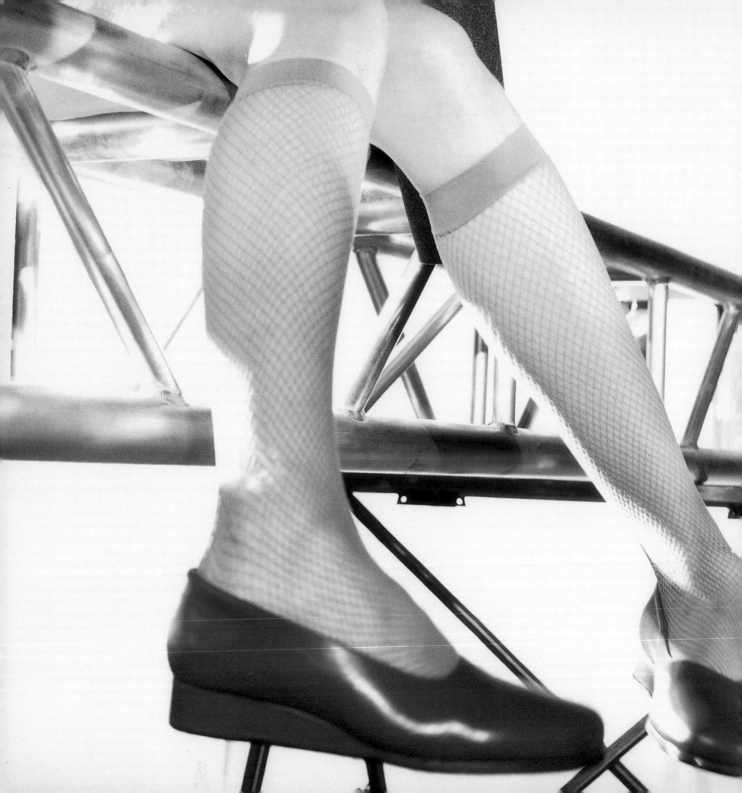

YOUR SHOES SAY A LOT ABOUT WHO YOU ARE. THINK ABOUT YOUR ELEMENTARY-SCHOOL PRINCIPAL. SHE WAS HARDLY THE SORT OF WOMAN WHO WORE SNAKESKIN, PEEPHOLE SLINGBACKS, NOW, WAS SHE? EVEN ON HER DAYS OFF. AND TAKE A LOOK AT YOUR OWN SHOES. ARE YOU A SENSIBLE, LACE-UP KIND OF GAL? DO YOU FAVOR HIGH HEELS WITH LOTS OF STRAPS? OR DO YOU LIKE TO SLOUCH AROUND IN A PAIR OF BIRKENSTOCK CLOGS? THE POINT ABOUT SHOES IS THE SHEER VARIETY AND CHOICE. AND THE CHANCES ARE THAT YOUR COLLECTION INCLUDES A PAIR OF TRAINERS AND SOMETHING GOLD AND FANCIFUL THAT YOU HAVE NEVER EVEN WORN.

IT IS NOT JUST WHAT YOU WEAR AND THE WAY YOU WEAR THEM; IT IS HOW YOU STORE THEM, TOO. SOME WOMEN HAVE THE LUXURY OF A SHOE CUPBOARD, DESIGNED SPECIFICALLY FOR THEIR HUNDRED PAIRS. OTHERS HAVE A BOX INTO WHICH THEIR SHOES ARE THROWN AFTER A NIGHT OUT. THEN THERE ARE THOSE WHO KEEP EACH PAIR IN ITS ORIGINAL BOX WITH A POLAROID OF THE SHOE STUCK ON THE FRONT. A PSYCHOLOGIST WOULD HAVE A FIELD DAY.

IF SHOES SAY SO MUCH ABOUT US, IT IS NO SURPRISE THAT WE ARE FASCINATED BY THE FOOTWEAR OF CELEBRITIES. IT IS THE SHOES OF THE RICH AND FAMOUS—STARS FROM THOSE PARALLEL PLANETS OF HOLLYWOOD, ROCK, AND POP—THAT SET TRENDS.

WHAT DO YOUR FREE LANCE WEDGES SAY ABOUT YOU? THEY SAY YOU ARE FUN-LOVING AND GLAMOROUS, BUT STILL HAVE YOUR FEET ON THE GROUND

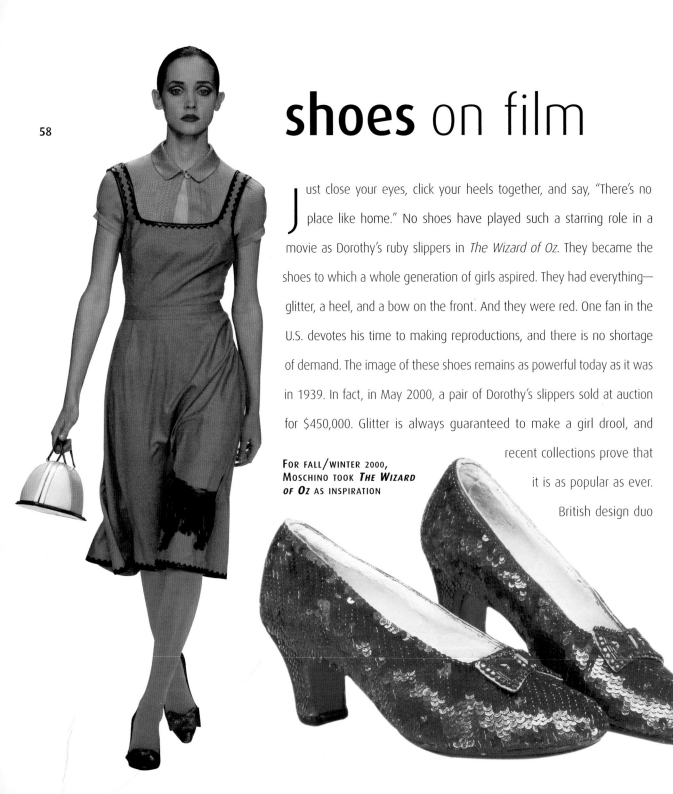

shoes on film

Just close your eyes, click your heels together, and say, "There's no place like home." No shoes have played such a starring role in a movie as Dorothy's ruby slippers in *The Wizard of Oz*. They became the shoes to which a whole generation of girls aspired. They had everything— glitter, a heel, and a bow on the front. And they were red. One fan in the U.S. devotes his time to making reproductions, and there is no shortage of demand. The image of these shoes remains as powerful today as it was in 1939. In fact, in May 2000, a pair of Dorothy's slippers sold at auction for $450,000. Glitter is always guaranteed to make a girl drool, and recent collections prove that it is as popular as ever. British design duo

FOR FALL/WINTER 2000, MOSCHINO TOOK *THE WIZARD OF OZ* AS INSPIRATION

Clements Ribeiro, for example, made their Manolos irresistibly sparkly. And when Italian fashion label Moschino showed a collection inspired by *The Wizard of Oz*, it planted pairs of stripy-stockinged legs, shod in ruby slippers, all around the catwalk theater. It is clear that they are still every girl—and boy's—fantasy shoe.

Children's fairytales often focus on the heroine's clothing. There was Little Red Riding Hood's cloak and, of course, Cinderella's glass slipper, which has appeared in countless movies, from MGM's 1955 all-singing, all-dancing version to the 1998 *Ever After*, starring Drew Barrymore. The slippers for *Ever After* were designed by Ferragamo who, from the start of his career, divided women into three categories: the Venus type, the Aristocrat type, and the Cinderella type. This last, he wrote, "takes a shoe smaller than a size six" and is a feminine person who loves

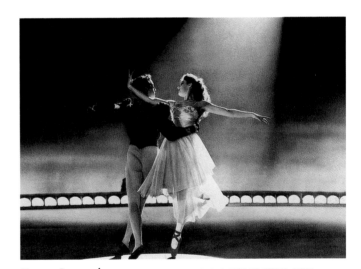

NORMA SHEARER'S RED SHOES OF 1948 HAD A LIFE OF THEIR OWN

jewels, furs, and being in love. The modern-day Cinderella would also, presumably, enjoy wearing Antonio Berardi's wooden clogs with jangling Venetian-glass flowers. Especially if they were presented to her on a velvet pillow by her Prince Charming.

The other Hans Christian Anderson fairytale based on a pair of shoes was *The Red Shoes*, which was made into a movie by Powell and Pressburger in 1948. The shoes in question were a pair of ballet pumps that had a life all of their own and, eventually, forced the heroine to cut off her feet to reclaim her life. In the movie, the red satin ballet shoes take control, and she throws herself into the path of an oncoming train. Ballet slippers have long been inspiration to shoe designers, from their chiseled toes, to the little bows at the front of flat pumps, to the ribbons that tie alluringly up the legs. Christian Louboutin gave his "toe shoes" heels and grosgrain ribbon, while the flat ballet pump has become a classic.

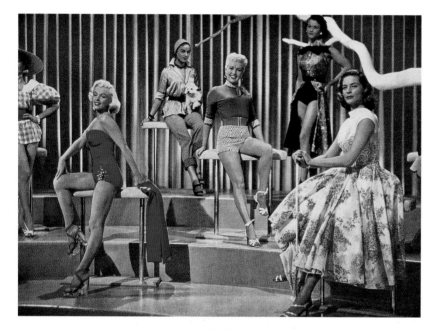

MARILYN MONROE KNEW HOW TO STRUT AND STRIKE A POSE IN A PAIR OF HIGH-HEELED SHOES

Other shoes that have appeared on the silver screen have been wanton and alluring. Marilyn Monroe is famously said to have had one of her heels cut shorter than the other to achieve her exaggerated, swinging hip movements. A painting by British artist Allen Jones was used for the poster for the 1976 movie *Maîtresse*, about a burglar who falls in love with a dominatrix. As always in his work, the shoes are symbolic and highly fetishized. Similarly, the Spanish filmmaker Pedro Almodóvar named one of his films *High Heels*, and the poster featured the star, Victoria Abril, in her stilettos, one of which has a smoking gun in place of a heel.

It would not be fair to talk about shoes on film without mentioning Minnie Mouse, the whimsical Walt Disney character who had a penchant for cute shoes. Everybody knows what is meant by "Minnie Mouse shoes"—the sort little girls like to dress up in, usually their mother's and five sizes too big. Believe it or not, they have been the inspiration for many a shoe designer. The American designer Marc Jacobs used Minnie's ears for his playful, flat pointies that look like a mouse's face, while Patrick Cox's Minnie Mouse peeptoe sandal for spring/summer 1986 was given a cartoon-like quality with an exaggerated leather bow— round like Minnie's ears—at the ankle. He was inspired by the minimal strokes of Walt's pen when he drew the shoes and confesses to being something of a child at heart. The roundness of a Disney cartoon shoe is, he says, friendly and encouraging. The shoes also give the wearer a touch of the character herself.

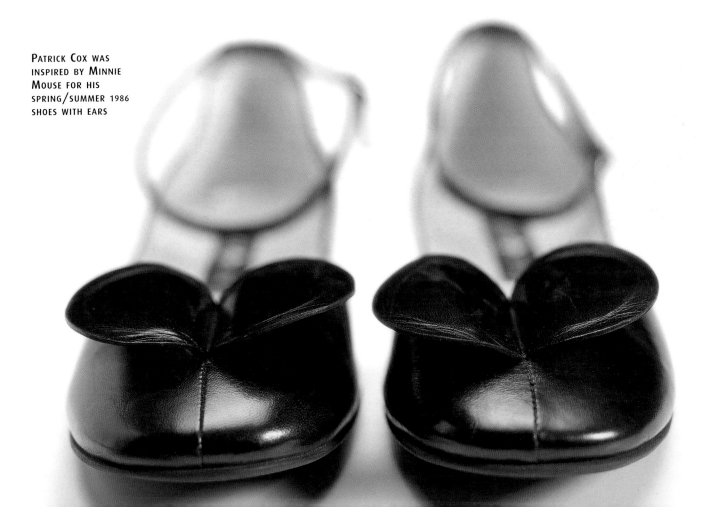

PATRICK COX WAS INSPIRED BY MINNIE MOUSE FOR HIS SPRING/SUMMER 1986 SHOES WITH EARS

the **imelda** syndrome

melda Marcos has a lot of things to be ashamed of, but her shoe collection is not one of them. She has been a role model to a whole generation of women who have set themselves up in competition with her, all vying to see if they can own as many—if not more—pairs of shoes. The difference, of course, is

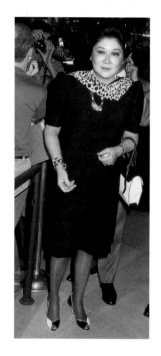

that on the whole they use their own money to feed their habit rather than that of their fellow citizens. "I did not have three thousand pairs of shoes, I had one thousand and sixty," she boasted in 1987. Ten years later, she asked, "What's wrong with shoes? I collected them because it was like a symbol of thanksgiving and love." As with any addiction, warped logic will justify anything. Her shoes, she claimed, were "very simple." Pumps. It just happened that she could wear a different pair every day for three years.

Shoes bring out the Imelda in a woman. It is a modern-day phenomenon. Like Karl Lagerfeld, who is said to wear a pair of underpants only once before throwing them away, Marlene Dietrich wore her shoes twice, at most. Only the latest style would do. And although Diana, Princess of Wales, was known to have close working relationships with many shoe designers—including Jimmy Choo, who kept the princess well heeled throughout the 1990s— she was by no means the first royal to take more than a passing interest in footwear. The Duchess of Windsor was quite a shoeaholic, ordering from Ferragamo on a regular basis— two-toned shoes for spring and summer, and solid-colored shoes for fall and winter.

So, who else wears what? You need only glance at the client list of London's Gina shoes to see a Who's Who of starry feet. The name Gina comes from Gina Lollabrigida. The

IMELDA MARCOS, ABOVE, IN JUST ONE OF HER 160,000 PAIRS OF SHOES. HELENA CHRISTENSEN, OPPOSITE, HAS AN UNFAIR ADVANTAGE— FANTASTIC LEGS AND ACCESS TO THE MOST FABULOUS SHOES

company was named for the Italian film star when it was launched in 1954. Kate Winslet has ordered Gina shoes, as did Diana, Princess of Wales. Madonna is a fan—on stage and off. Nicole Kidman and Jade Jagger ordered Gina shoes, as did Sophie Rhys Jones for her wedding to Prince Edward. Meg Matthews, a woman who loves to shop almost as much as she loves shoes, is a regular, along with Kylie Minogue and Kate Moss. Even the ballerina Darcy Bussell has been known to indulge in Gina. However, she does not have quite the reputation of the prima ballerina before her, Alicia Markova, who took two trunks filled with heels wherever she traveled.

Models have a reputation for collecting shoes. But then, they have better access to the world's most elegant and glamorous shoes than the rest of us. It is not unusual for a model to be spotted wearing a designer prototype as much as a full season before they are put into production. It is one of the perks of the job. No one is going to say "No" to Naomi if, backstage at a show, she takes a shine to a pair of must-have shoes. Similarly, it is not surprising that Kate Moss, Helena Christensen, and Claudia Schiffer have some of the fanciest footwork in the business.

The shopping habits of British socialites Tara Palmer-Tomkinson and Tamara Beckwith are well documented. Manolo is their first port of call, followed by Gina, Gucci, Prada, Sergio Rossi, Dolce e Gabbana, Jimmy Choo … anywhere they can buy a sexy shoe with a high heel and a pointed toe. Posh Spice has quite a sweet tooth when it comes to shoes, too. She is a fool for Manolo, but is rarely photographed wearing the same pair twice. So, too, Elizabeth Hurley, although her favorite is Versace, if only because it is her most successful one-stop shop. Any dress split to the hip requires something special on the feet to balance the look.

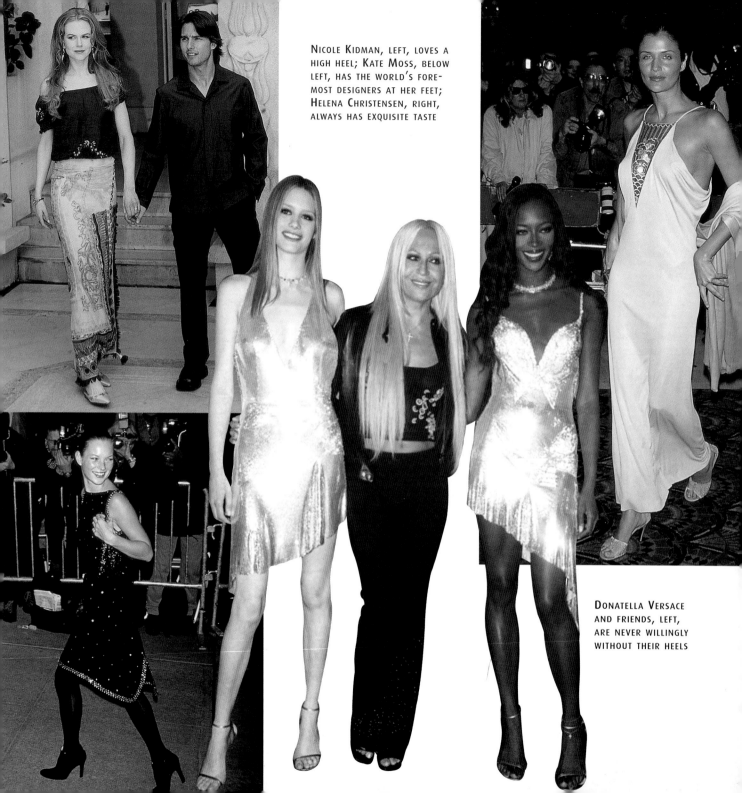

NICOLE KIDMAN, LEFT, LOVES A HIGH HEEL; KATE MOSS, BELOW LEFT, HAS THE WORLD'S FOREMOST DESIGNERS AT HER FEET; HELENA CHRISTENSEN, RIGHT, ALWAYS HAS EXQUISITE TASTE

DONATELLA VERSACE AND FRIENDS, LEFT, ARE NEVER WILLINGLY WITHOUT THEIR HEELS

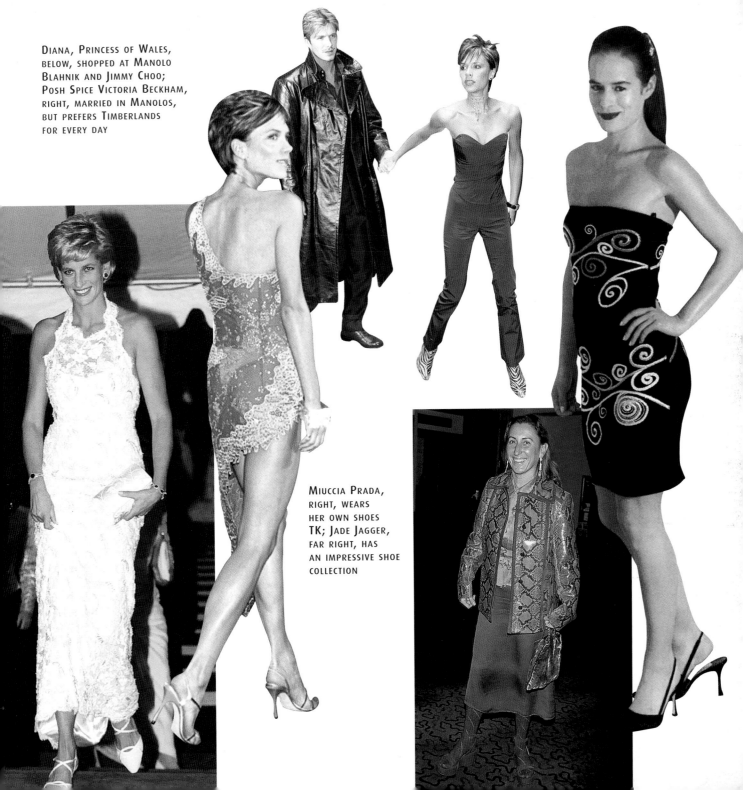

DIANA, PRINCESS OF WALES,
BELOW, SHOPPED AT MANOLO
BLAHNIK AND JIMMY CHOO;
POSH SPICE VICTORIA BECKHAM,
RIGHT, MARRIED IN MANOLOS,
BUT PREFERS TIMBERLANDS
FOR EVERY DAY

MIUCCIA PRADA,
RIGHT, WEARS
HER OWN SHOES
TK; JADE JAGGER,
FAR RIGHT, HAS
AN IMPRESSIVE SHOE
COLLECTION

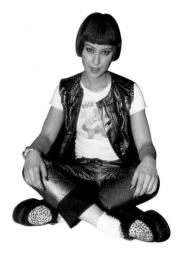

Sex, drugs, rock'n'roll ... and silly shoes. Ever since Elvis and his blue suede shoes, and the Beatles and their "winklepickers," many popular trends in footwear have started with rock'n'roll. Elvis famously sang about shoes, his own blue-suede crepe soles becoming a symbol of all that was rebellious and teenaged in the middle of the twentieth century. The blue suedes had thick crepe soles,

SAFFRON OF REPUBLICA, ABOVE, REFUSES TO WEAR ANYTHING BUT CREEPERS ON HER FEET; LI'L KIM IS PRETTY IN PINK, VERSACE "ROCK STYLE", RIGHT; IN THE 1970S ELTON JOHN'S SHOES GOT HIGHER AND HIGHER, OPPOSITE TOP; TINA TURNER MANAGES TO STRUT HER STUFF IN THE SPIKIEST OF HEELS, OPPOSITE BOTTOM

the forerunner, perhaps, of the Buffalo platforms of the 1990s, and were part of the uniform of the teddy boys in the 1950s. Crepe-soled shoes are still made today and have become a design classic. Saffron, the scarlet-haired singer from the British band Republica, rarely performs without hers. Even when she was invited by Donatella Versace to perform a live set during a Versus show in New York, Saffron refused to don the high heels intended for her black leather "rock chick" outfit and insisted on wearing her beloved "creepers."

rock 'n' shoes

In the 1970s P-funk star Bootsy Collins made ridiculous boots into an art form, and Elton John became known as much for his gravity-defying platforms as for his music. To perform in the rock musical *Tommy*, he

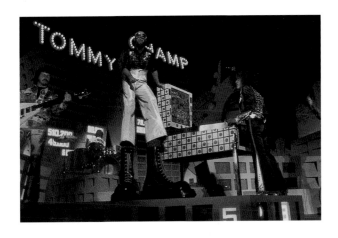

continued to play with his trademark by wearing the biggest Doc Marten boots in the world. With every performance, his outfit—and shoes—would get more and more extreme. Along with Gary Glitter, who was the leader of the stack-shoe gang, Elton defined a decade of shoes.

In the 1980s girl groups like Bananarama wore Doc Martens. In fact, everyone wore Doc Martens. Punks wore them. Mods wore them. Madness made London's Camden shoe shop famous for them. Even the soul singer Sade wore them. And then came rap and hiphop, and the only possible footwear was Adidas.

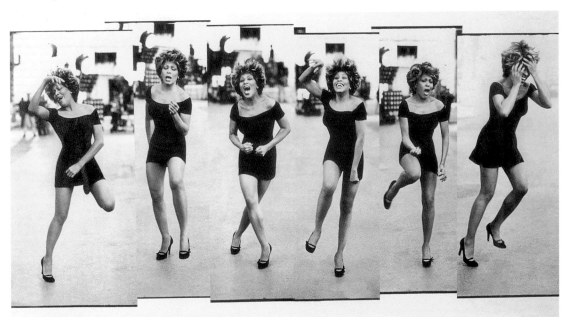

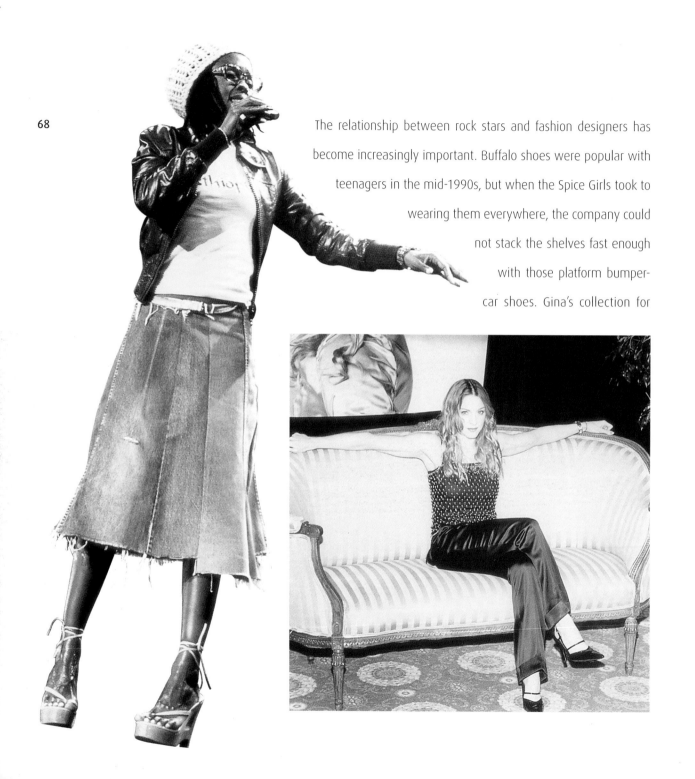

The relationship between rock stars and fashion designers has become increasingly important. Buffalo shoes were popular with teenagers in the mid-1990s, but when the Spice Girls took to wearing them everywhere, the company could not stack the shelves fast enough with those platform bumper-car shoes. Gina's collection for fall/winter 2000—2001 was called Rock Star and featured boots for evening in fabrics like shiny python skin, and embossed velvet, and with heels encrusted with jewels. No wonder Tina Turner, Skin from Skunk Anansie, and Jennifer Lopez all shop there. Madonna wore hers for the video of "American Pie." Singers like Lauryn Hill and Missie Elliott are the fashion icons of our time, and John Galliano certainly thinks so. He dedicated a collection to Foxy Brown and Ms. Hill, making knee-high distressed denim boots for Christian Dior with the music queens in mind. He has taken music subcultures as his reference point for other collections before, starting with rock'n'roll bobby soxers and their spikes, taking in punks with bondage boots, two-tone mods with pointed toes, and even a nod toward Leigh Bowery and the excesses of the 1980s London club scene. Even Rei Kawakubo has come over all punk, with leather bondage boots.

Dolce e Gabbana and Gucci both cultivate the music scene: D&G with Madonna and Gucci's Tom Ford paying homage to Cher. But Versace is the label for the rock glitterati. The Versace book *Rock and Royalty* makes little differentiation between Prince Charles and, well, Prince. Except that (the Artist Fromerly Known as) Prince wears a pair of purple pixie boots with a high heel and a side zipper. If you want to look—and feel—like a rock star, a pair of snakeskin heels or something with a rhinestone buckle is all you need. Sandy Shaw, of course, made a virtue of wearing no shoes at all.

LAURYN HILL, OPPOSITE LEFT, ALWAYS LOOKS COOL, FROM HER HEAD TO HER FEET; MADONNA, OPPOSITE RIGHT, SAYS HER MANOLOS LAST MUCH LONGER THAN SEX; SANDIE SHAW, BELOW, ALWAYS PREFERRED TO GO BAREFOOT

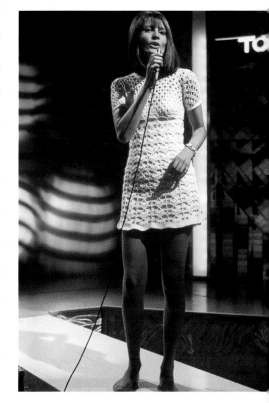

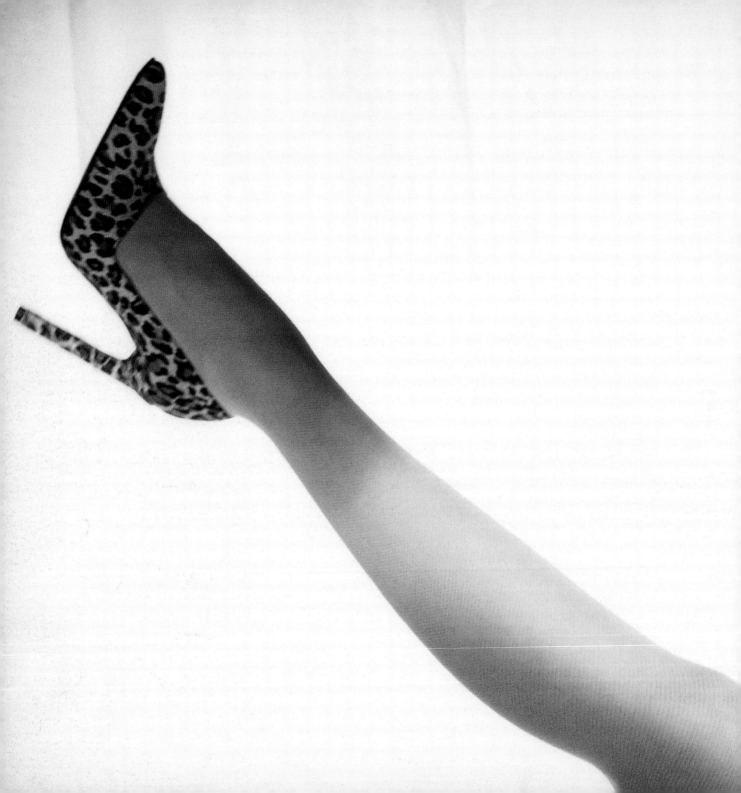

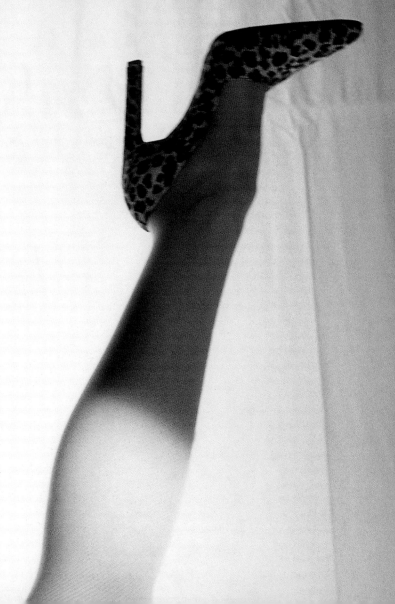

chapter 3
THE **A–Z** OF SHOES

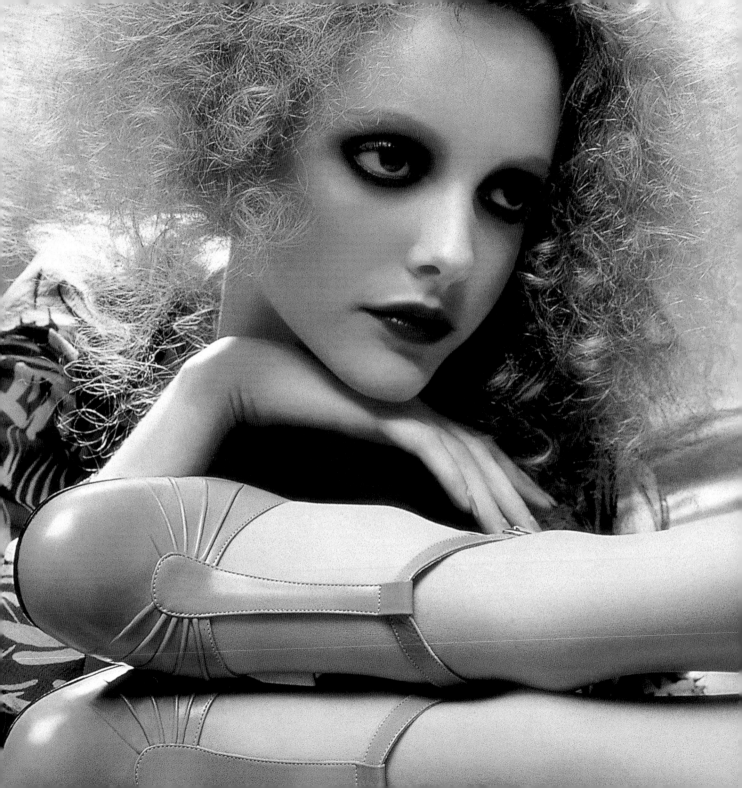

THERE ARE SOME WOMEN WHO FILE THEIR SHOE COLLECTIONS ALPHABETICALLY. THEY MIGHT BEGIN AT "B" FOR BLAHNIK (THE SORT OF WOMAN WHO GOES TO THESE LENGTHS HAS SO MANY BLAHNIKS YOU WOULD THINK SHE WAS A CENTIPEDE) AND END AT "V" FOR VIVIER. THEY ARE LOVINGLY STORED IN BOXES WITH A LABEL AND A LITTLE POLAROID FOR EASY VIEWING. WHEN SHE ONLY HAS HALF AN HOUR TO GET DRESSED TO GO OUT FOR AN EVENING AT THE THEATER OR A DINNER PARTY, IT IS IMPORTANT THAT SHE CAN ACCESS HER HUGE COLLECTION OF SHOES AS QUICKLY AND EFFICIENTLY AS POSSIBLE. THE REAL SHOE LOVER IS AS FANATICAL ABOUT HER SHOES AS HER PARTNER MIGHT BE ABOUT HIS CD COLLECTION. EVEN IF THE SHOES ARE NOT CATALOGUED BY DESIGNER, IT WOULD BE UNHEARD OF SIMPLY TO LEAVE THEM IN A PILE UNDER THE BED. SHOES, YOU SEE, MUST BE TREATED WITH THE UTMOST RESPECT. SO WHAT WILL IT BE? "G" FOR GUCCI? "P" FOR PRADA? OR "C" FOR COX? HAPPY FILING.

C IS FOR COX: PATRICK COX, THE LONDON-BASED SHOE DESIGNER WHOSE COLLECTION RANGES FROM THE **WANNABE** LOAFER FOR DAY, TO THE MOST ELEGANT HIGH-HEELED SHOES FOR EVENING

74

PAUL ANDREW

British designer Paul Andrew is a name to watch. In summer 1999 his graduation collection was snapped up by Yasmin Cho, the hip London boutique. His shoes have a pleasing shape and balance— glamorous and sexy, yet functional, too. Following interviews in New York, Andrew accepted a position designing shoes and accessories for the New York-based designer Narciso Rodriguez, renowned for having designed Carolyn Bessette Kennedy's wedding dress in 1996. The highly rated graduation collection included a pair of gold high-heel sandals that laced around the leg. His first accessories collection for Rodriguez hits the shops in fall 2000, with shoes which Andrews describes as inspired by "toe caps and spectator shoes. Skinny heels, pointy toes and very sexy."

PAUL ANDREW SOLD HIS GRADUATION COLLECTION TO LONDON BOUTIQUE YASMIN CHO

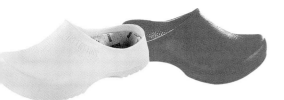

BIRKENSTOCK

The Birkenstock story begins in 1754, when Johann Adam Birkenstock was born in Germany. Registered in the Church archives as "citizen and shoemaker," he was first in a long line of cobblers. In 1896 Konrad Birkenstock produced footbed soles specially designed to cradle and nurture the foot, and he created orthopedic footwear for soldiers wounded in the World War I. Konrad, Jr., joined the company in 1925 and bought a larger factory to make the Blue Footbed around the clock to meet European demand. By the 1940s the BIrkenstock name was synonymous with foot health and was supported by leading doctors. In 1969 the cork sole was produced, and the Birkenstock sandal also became a fashion statement, albeit a hippie one. Birkenstock continued to grow, and in the 1990s the clog was favored by fashion groupies, art school students, and nightclubbers. Affectionately known as the "Birkie," it is considered an eco-friendly, functional design classic. Thongs, sandals, and clogs were made in bright colors and different fabrics. By the mid-1990s the clog was widely copied, and even the plastic gardening shoe became cult footwear. American designer Narciso Rodriguez asked Birkenstock to produce cashmere clogs for his first own-name luxurious collection. For once, there's a fashion shoe that is good for your feet.

BIRKENSTOCK'S TRADEMARK IS ITS
REVOLUTIONARY FOOTBED, DESIGNED
FOR MAXIMUM COMFORT

MANOLO BLAHNIK

Just one single word is all it takes: Manolo. There is no need for a last name, no need to ask Manolo who? Manolo is quite simply the last name in luxury shoes. His would be the name inside Cinderella's shoes. His is the name inside the shoes of most of the world's princesses and celebrities. Mention the name Manolo, and you conjure up images of elegant high-heeled slippers, the sort of shoes that were never made for walking. These shoes come with a built-in bill for a limo and chauffeur, or at least a taxi

THIS STRIPY-HEEL MULE IS TYPICAL OF MANOLO BLAHNIK'S EFFORTLESS WIT AND ELEGANCE

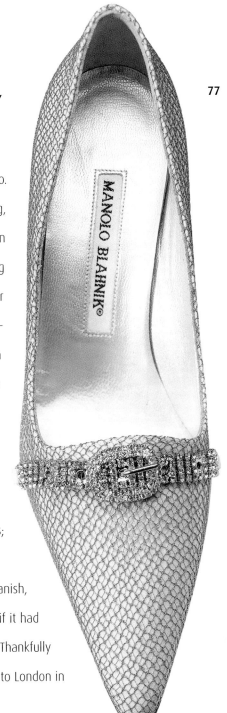

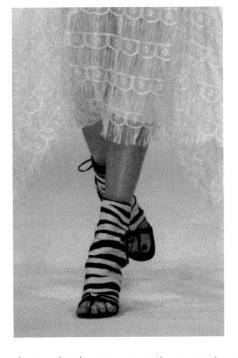

A ZEBRA-PRINT GLADIATOR SANDAL, LEFT, BY MANOLO BLAHNIK, FOR BRITISH DESIGN DUO CLEMENTS RIBEIRO. ANOTHER EXAMPLE OF BLAHNIK'S EYE FOR LUXURY, RIGHT

and driver wherever you go. They are too good for walking, too grand to risk getting wet in the rain, to push a shopping cart around a supermarket, or to scuff on harsh city streets— although there are women who do all of this and more in their Manolos. They are designed to be worn on antique carpets, or simply dangling from the toes of a fashion editor seated in the front row at a fashion show. No self-respecting lover of shoes would be without a pair. Even if they are beyond your budget—a pair will set you back over $300—there are always the sales; and if your size has already sold out, there are banks to rob.

Manolo Blahnik was born in 1942 in the Canary Islands. He is part Spanish, part Czech (hence the exotic name), and was born to create. He says that if it had not been shoes, he would have created hats, or art, or sculpture, or fashion. Thankfully for his fans the world over, he fell into the craft of shoemaking. He moved to London in

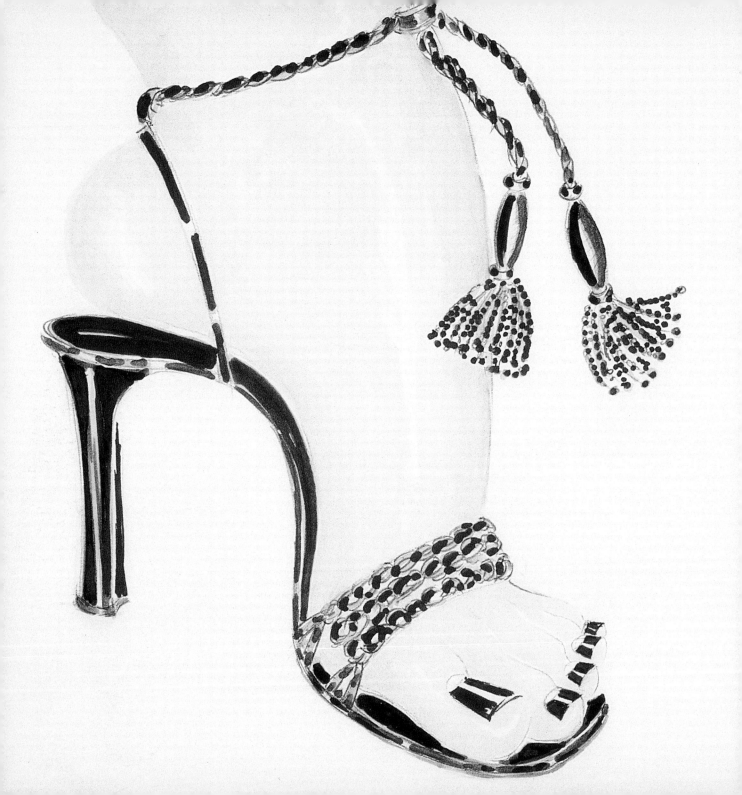

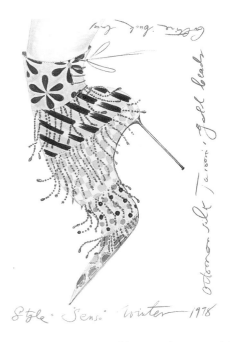

Style Senso Winter 1978

MANOLO BLAHNIK'S SKETCHES, LEFT,
ARE SO FULL OF LIFE AND COLOR
THEY ARE USED IN HIS ADVERTISING.
A PAIR SANDALS THAT LACE UP THE
LEG, RIGHT, FOR CLEMENTS RIBEIRO

1972 and made his first shoes for the designer Ossie Clark in that year. Since then his customers have included Bianca Jagger, Diana Ross, Kate Moss, the late Diana, Princess of Wales and Madonna. He works from his studio on London's King's Road, still making the last (the wood or metal form on which every shoe or boot is fashioned) of every shoe that bares his name. In addition to his own collection, he makes shoes for a whole host of design houses, including John Galliano, Christian Dior, Antonio Berardi, and Clements Ribeiro. For Dior, he recently created the most fabulous high-heel shoes, encrusted with "diamonds" inside their heels. The mirrored catwalk was made to show off the underneath of the shoes, which were as luxurious as the uppers. For Antonio Berardi, he created shoes made of gold, costing $25,000 a pair, that had to travel to the show venue with a security guard. And for a Clements Ribeiro collection, he created a series of shoes covered in sparkling glitter. Madonna remains a loyal fan, saying that his shoes are wonderful because they "last longer than sex."

CAMPER

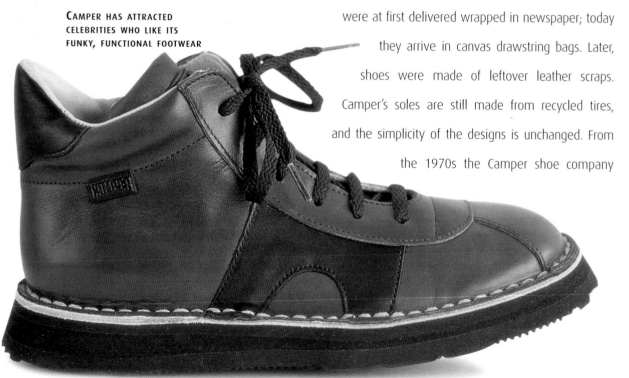

In 1975 the Majorcan family-run shoe company began to manufacture Camaleón, a rough-and-ready shoe that was already part of the local landscape and culture. A collection mainstay, it has been produced since the early 1900s by Majorcan countrymen. Truck tires were used for soles, stitched on to a basic canvas upper with hemp thread, with string for laces. A design classic, Camaleón is ecologically sound and uses recycled materials. Utterly practical, the shoes

CAMPER HAS ATTRACTED CELEBRITIES WHO LIKE ITS FUNKY, FUNCTIONAL FOOTWEAR

were at first delivered wrapped in newspaper; today they arrive in canvas drawstring bags. Later, shoes were made of leftover leather scraps. Camper's soles are still made from recycled tires, and the simplicity of the designs is unchanged. From the 1970s the Camper shoe company

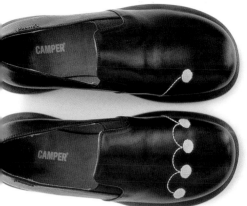

expanded internationally, and among their hip clientele are the Gallagher brothers. Renowned graphic designer Neville Brody was also appointed art director.

Brilliantly designed, each store is a totally different environment, with shoes displayed so that they can be picked up and admired without any pressure to try them on. London's first store, which opened in Covent Garden in 1995, is an industrial affair of cool stainless steel, while the tiny New Bond Street branch features a Velcro wall designed so that shoes can be easily pulled off. Camper's designers focus on trendsetting shoes. The Mix line uses state-of-the-art fabrics like bulletproof Kevlar, while the Cloud is feather-light. Twins features odd shoes, mismatched laces, or different heels . Cartujano uses traditional shoemaking and leather crafts of southern Spain, usually reserved for all things equestrian.

CAMPER'S SHOES STAND OUT BECAUSE OF THEIR ODDBALL DESIGNS, INCLUDING ITS TWINS LINE OF MISMATCHING SHOES. THE STORES ALL HAVE DIFFERENT DESIGNS, TOO, MAKING BUYING SHOES AT CAMPER AS MUCH FUN AS ACTUALLY WEARING THE SHOES

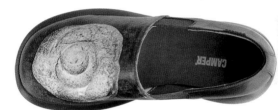

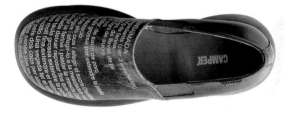

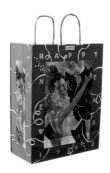
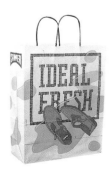
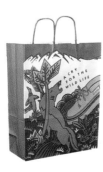
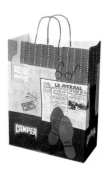
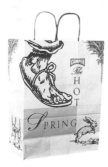

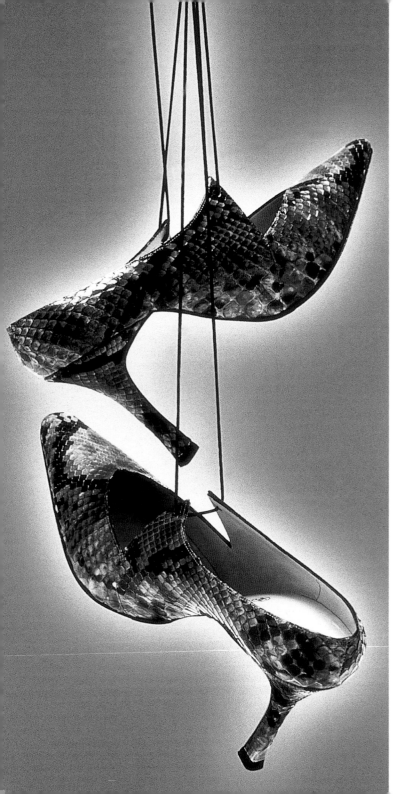

CHANEL

Think Chanel and you will most likely imagine the classic tweed suit that Coco Chanel designed in the 1920s and which Karl Lagerfeld still manages to make modern today. You will think of Chanel No. 5, one of the most successful perfumes of all time. And you may also conjure up the two-tone slingback pumps that are designed to elongate the leg, to be discreet and comfortable, and never date.

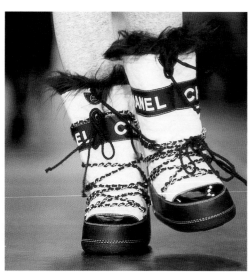

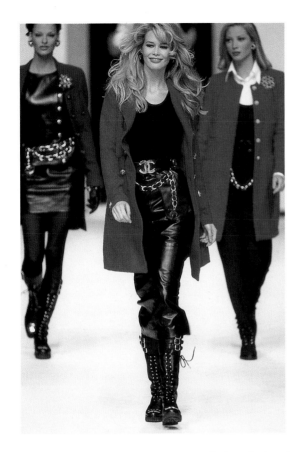

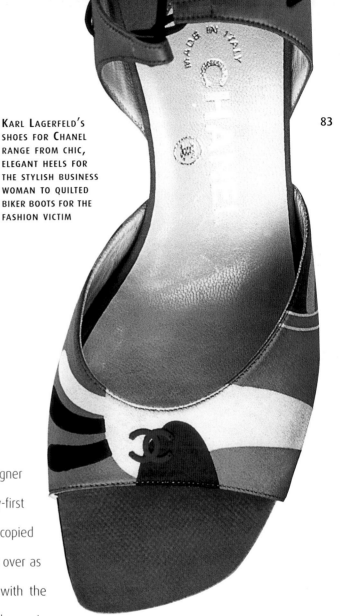

**KARL LAGERFELD'S
SHOES FOR CHANEL
RANGE FROM CHIC,
ELEGANT HEELS FOR
THE STYLISH BUSINESS
WOMAN TO QUILTED
BIKER BOOTS FOR THE
FASHION VICTIM**

These elegant shoes became symbolic of the designer 1980s, but have survived to be worn in the twenty-first century. They are undeniably Chanel and have been copied in chain stores everywhere. Since Karl Lagerfeld took over as head designer in 1983, he has played incessantly with the Chanel logo and its trademark designs. Footwear has been given the full treatment. He has made quilted biker boots, prim navy-and-white pumps, flip-flops decorated with the classic gold chains, high heels embellished with the signature camellia, trainers, futuristic Star Trek sandals, moon boots—even galoshes, Chanel style, in Day-Glo pink.

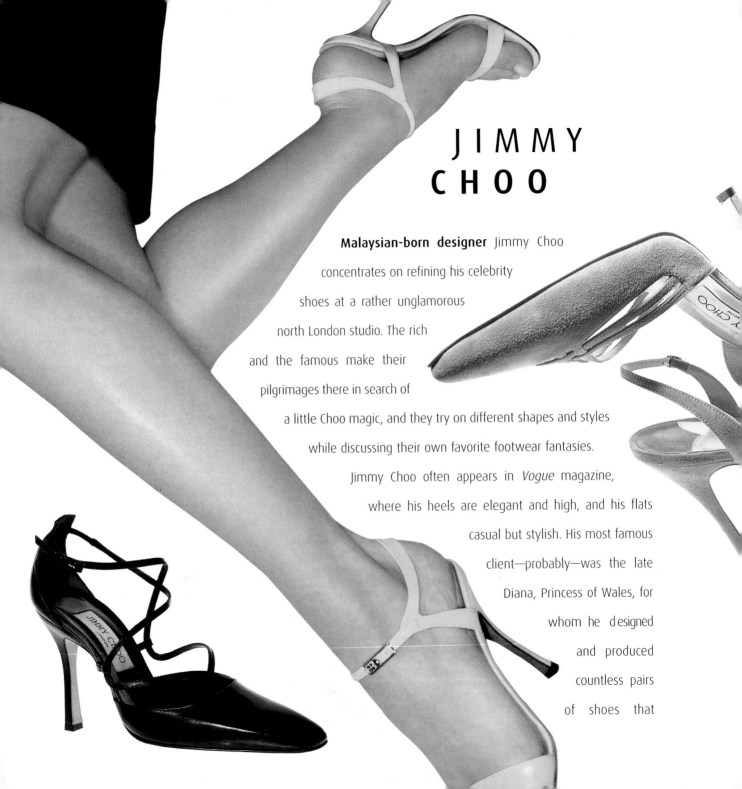

JIMMY CHOO

Malaysian-born designer Jimmy Choo concentrates on refining his celebrity shoes at a rather unglamorous north London studio. The rich and the famous make their pilgrimages there in search of a little Choo magic, and they try on different shapes and styles while discussing their own favorite footwear fantasies. Jimmy Choo often appears in *Vogue* magazine, where his heels are elegant and high, and his flats casual but stylish. His most famous client—probably—was the late Diana, Princess of Wales, for whom he designed and produced countless pairs of shoes that

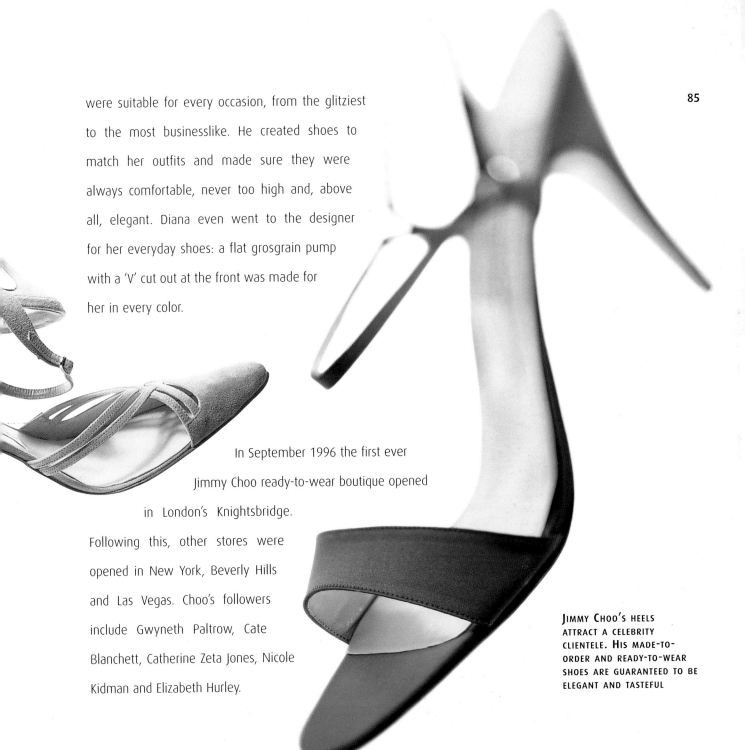

were suitable for every occasion, from the glitziest to the most businesslike. He created shoes to match her outfits and made sure they were always comfortable, never too high and, above all, elegant. Diana even went to the designer for her everyday shoes: a flat grosgrain pump with a 'V' cut out at the front was made for her in every color.

In September 1996 the first ever Jimmy Choo ready-to-wear boutique opened in London's Knightsbridge. Following this, other stores were opened in New York, Beverly Hills and Las Vegas. Choo's followers include Gwyneth Paltrow, Cate Blanchett, Catherine Zeta Jones, Nicole Kidman and Elizabeth Hurley.

JIMMY CHOO'S HEELS ATTRACT A CELEBRITY CLIENTELE. HIS MADE-TO-ORDER AND READY-TO-WEAR SHOES ARE GUARANTEED TO BE ELEGANT AND TASTEFUL

ADELE CLARKE

CLARKE HAS DESIGNED FOR HUSSEIN CHALAYAN BUT HAS YET TO PUT HER OWN COLLECTION IN PRODUCTION

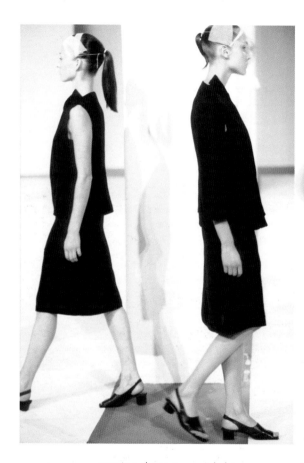

Unrelated to

the "desert boot" Clarks, Adele Clarke graduated in 1999 from London's Royal College of Art; she was the only footwear designer to graduate in that year. For Clarke, shoes are as much about concept as they are about sex appeal or heel height. She has worked for several seasons with the British Designer of the Year 2000, Hussein Chalayan, creating shoes to match his sparse, perfectly executed clothing. At first glance her designs are plain and classic, but a closer look will always reveal some sort of twist. For Chalayan, she made shoes that are perfectly symmetrical when the feet are positioned side by side. Her's is a talent to watch.

CLARKS

An all-time classic, the Clarks' Desert Boot was designed in 1945 by Nathan Clark while he was serving in the army in the Sahara desert. Clark had seen officers wearing crepe-soled boots (sold in the Cairo bazaar) which were suitable for the hot, dry, sandy conditions. In 1950 he launched his desert boot (an instant hit) at the Chicago Shoe Fair. Part of the student beatnik brigade uniform in Europe, it was quickly adopted in the U.S. as the cool man's casual shoe and was worn by Andy Warhol. A recognized footwear icon, the style still remains unchanged. Today's fans include Paul Weller and Liam Gallagher (who got married in his). The Desert Boot and the Wallabee, another design first introduced in 1965, have achieved international cult status. The Wallabee, acclaimed as "the world's ugliest shoe" by Blakes in Los Angeles, has been adopted by West Coast rap artists, the Wu Tang Clan, who customize theirs. Based in Somerset, England, Clarks continues to make middle-of-the-road, mass-market shoes for their loyal customers, but the original Desert Boot deserves its place in New York's Metropolitan Museum of Art.

CLARKS' DESERT BOOT IS OVER HALF A CENTURY OLD BUT LOOKS AS MODERN TODAY AS IT DID ORIGINALLY

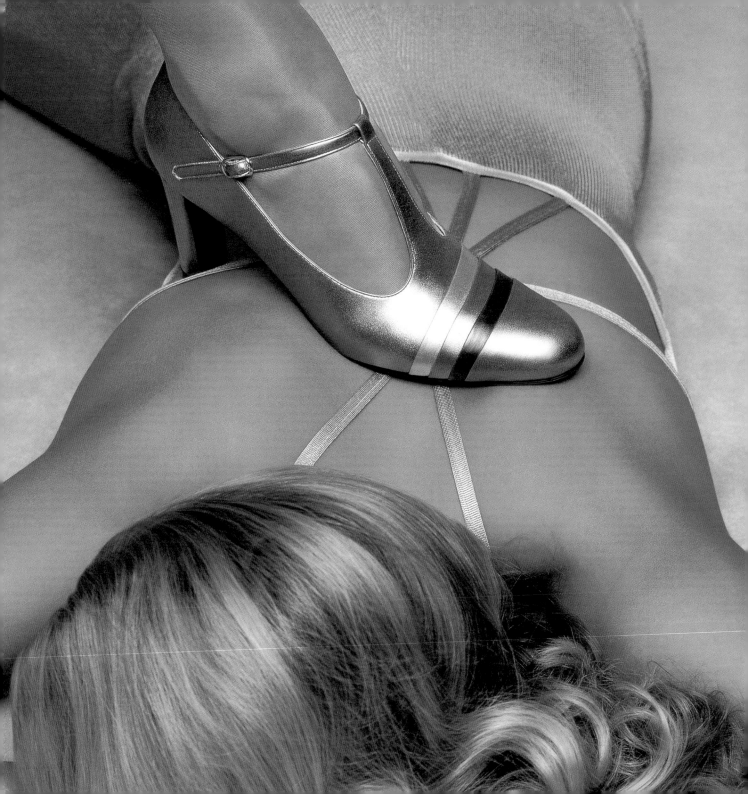

PATRICK COX

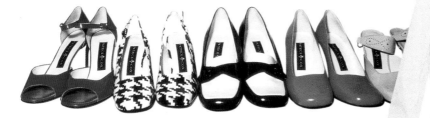

Canadian-born designer Patrick Cox moved to England in 1983 to attend east London's famous Cordwainers College. Before he had even graduated, he was designing shoes for Vivienne Westwood and the influential 1980s design duo Bodymap. After graduating, he worked on shoes for John Galliano's "Fallen Angels" show in 1986 and created the famous Hobo boot, which was all patched up and apparently falling apart. Cox went on to set up his own

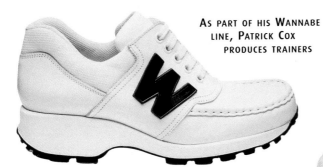

AS PART OF HIS WANNABE LINE, PATRICK COX PRODUCES TRAINERS

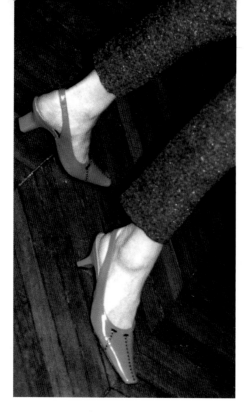

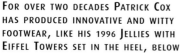

FOR OVER TWO DECADES PATRICK COX HAS PRODUCED INNOVATIVE AND WITTY FOOTWEAR, LIKE HIS 1996 JELLIES WITH EIFFEL TOWERS SET IN THE HEEL, BELOW

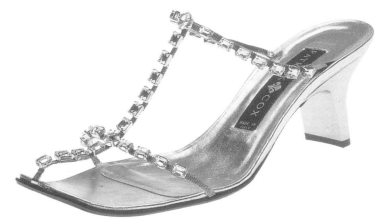

business, continuing to supplement his income and boost his profile by designing for leading London designers of the day, including John Flett, Workers for Freedom, and Richard James. In 1991 he opened his own store in London's Chelsea, followed by one in Paris in 1993 (the same year that he was awarded Accessory Designer of the Year by the British Fashion Council). Unique in his ability to straddle with ease the worlds of high glamour and ready-to-wear, Cox launched the Wannabe loafer in 1995, and a secondary, more accessible line of footwear with sharp Cox styling was born. It became an instant hit, attracting Patrick Cox main-label wannabes, as well as those who could afford the main collection. This one shoe—in all its style variations—has given British men a new aim in

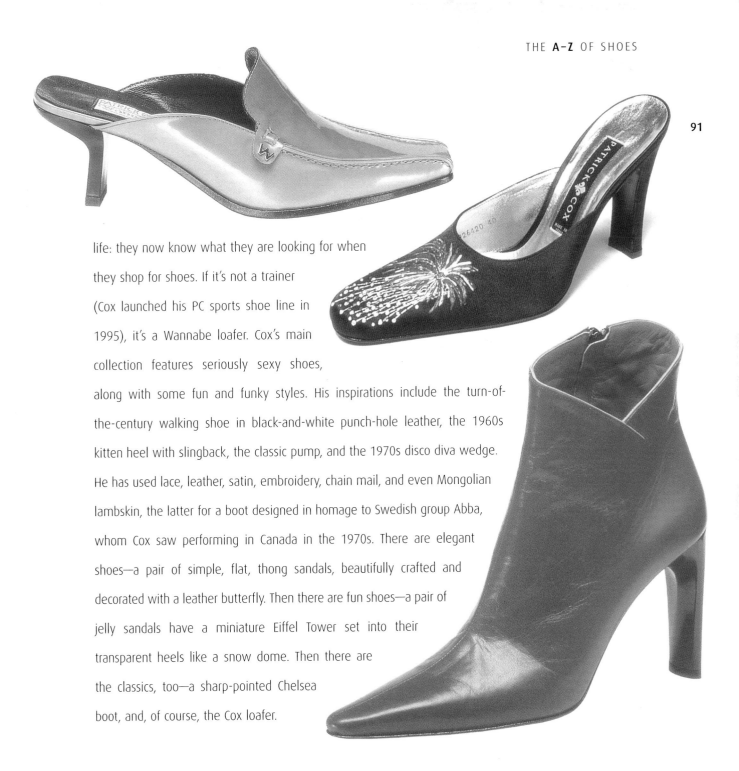

life: they now know what they are looking for when they shop for shoes. If it's not a trainer (Cox launched his PC sports shoe line in 1995), it's a Wannabe loafer. Cox's main collection features seriously sexy shoes, along with some fun and funky styles. His inspirations include the turn-of-the-century walking shoe in black-and-white punch-hole leather, the 1960s kitten heel with slingback, the classic pump, and the 1970s disco diva wedge. He has used lace, leather, satin, embroidery, chain mail, and even Mongolian lambskin, the latter for a boot designed in homage to Swedish group Abba, whom Cox saw performing in Canada in the 1970s. There are elegant shoes—a pair of simple, flat, thong sandals, beautifully crafted and decorated with a leather butterfly. Then there are fun shoes—a pair of jelly sandals have a miniature Eiffel Tower set into their transparent heels like a snow dome. Then there are the classics, too—a sharp-pointed Chelsea boot, and, of course, the Cox loafer.

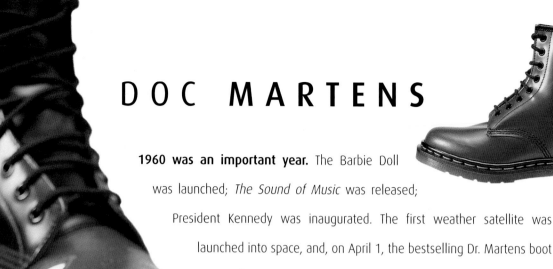

DOC MARTENS

1960 was an important year. The Barbie Doll was launched; *The Sound of Music* was released; President Kennedy was inaugurated. The first weather satellite was launched into space, and, on April 1, the bestselling Dr. Martens boot (known as the 1460) was born in Wollaston in the English Midlands. Over 40 years on, family-run company R. Griggs makes over one million pairs of boots monthly. Believe it or not, Dr. Martens really existed, along with his partner Dr. Herbert Funck. Dr. Maertens (a German) invented the world's first heat-sealed, air-cushioned sole. Griggs became the exclusive manufacturer and named it (without the first "e") after the inventor. Known as "bovver boots," long-lasting, affordable Dr.

The Doc Martens brand has developed from workwear into a fashion icon of the late twentieth century

Martens became a symbol of aggression and antisocial behavior. They were adopted by 1960s Mods, 1970s Skinheads, and 1980s art students, indie kids, and grunge followers, as well as almost every subculture known to man, from punks to hippies, who painted them in rainbow colors and added brightly colored laces. In Japan they have achieved cult status. Gwen Stefani has hers custom-made. Doc Martens continue to be worn in workplaces around the world.

DR. SCHOLL

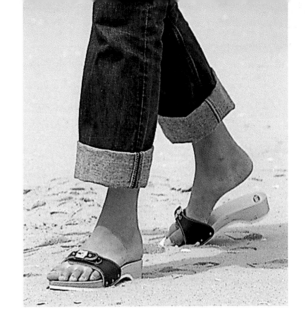

A STILL-STRONG FAVORITE FROM THE 1960S AND 1970S, DR. SCHOLL'S SANDALS ARE ACTUALLY GOOD FOR YOU— THEY EXERCISE YOUR LEG MUSCLES AS YOU WALK

In a similar way to Birkenstock clogs and Doc Martens boots, Dr. Scholl's exercise sandals have slipped into the unlikely role of fashion icon without any effort at all. The sandals were never intended to be anything more than wooden-soled shoes, which were designed to exercise all your calf muscles while you did the housework or walked to the local store. However, as is often the way, they have become a firm fashion favorite; a cheap sandal, worn tongue in cheek. Dr. Scholl's are the headscarves of the shoe world. They are the sort of shoes you would expect to see royalty wearing on their days off, instead of on the feet of fashionistas clipclopping into the coolest nightclubs in town. The unique appeal of the Dr. Scholl exercise sandal lies in its very frumpiness. It was invented by Dr. William Scholl in Chicago in 1962 and was sold, along with cough mixtures, support hose, and aspirins, in drugstores. The main market for the shoes throughout the 1960s and 1970s was housewives and waitresses, who thought they might as well exercise their leg muscles as they worked. Dr. Scholls also had a certain hippie appeal since they were simple, low tech and inexpensive. In 1994 American designers Isaac Mizrahi and Michael Kors took the Dr. Scholl onto the international catwalks, and even Gap put their own copycat version into production. Nothing quite beats the real thing, however, although the rest of the Dr. Scholl line remains firmly rooted in the orthopedic camp, well away from the fickle world of fashion.

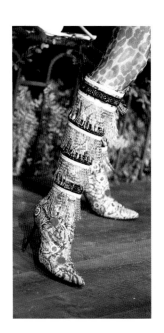

DOLCE E GABBANA

DOLCE E GABBANA'S SHOES ALWAYS REFLECT THE SEASON'S FASHION TREND

For Italian design duo Dolce e Gabbana, shoes are an extension of their overall vision for every collection. If the collection that year features shiny hologram fabric dresses coated in see-through plastic, then the shoes will be a microversion of that. Camden Market hippie? Then you must take a look at the patchwork boots. Butterfly-print cocktail dress? The shoes are guaranteed to match. Gangster suits? There's the perfect pair of men's lace-ups for women. A quick glance through the company's shoe archives will give an overview of every collection since their inception in 1985. An utterly mad mix of gold brocade heels, hooker-style shoes decorated with brash flowers, clashing colors and sparkly crystal pumps says it all.

DOLCE E GABBANA'S HOLOGRAM SHOES ARE TYPICAL OF THEIR FUN AND FANCIFUL ATTITUDE TOWARD SHOES

FENDI

The Fendi sisters, who recently sold a percentage of their business to Prada, have been in business since just after World War II, when they joined the family company set up by their brothers in 1925. Since then, their double-F logo has become easily one of the most recognizable in fashion. Fendi's phenomenal success with the covetable baguette bag (there are waiting

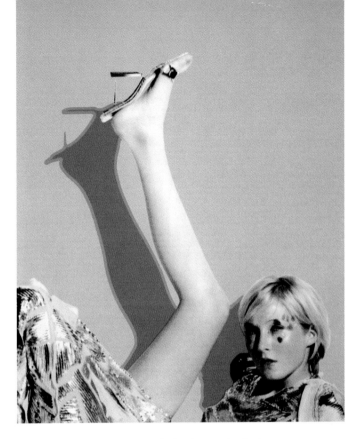

lists wherever it is sold) has catapulted them right back into the fashion spotlight under the ever-watchful eye of design guru Karl Lagerfeld. The logo mania of 1999 and 2000 has meant that Fendi is one of the most fashionable labels money can buy, whether it appears on a bag, a belt, a scarf, or—of course—a pair of shoes. With the logo printed on the canvas, Fendi's trainers will surely become future collector's items, both precious and throwaway at the same time.

FENDI SHOES ARE AS DESIRABLE AS
THE LUXURY COMPANY'S HANDBAGS

FERRAGAMO

In October 1999 Ferragamo, the Italian family-run shoe and fashion house, bought a pair of shoes at Christie's in New York. The shoes belonged to Marilyn Monroe and were made for her by the Neapolitan-born Salvatore Ferragamo, who founded his company as a teenager. Before the outbreak of World War I, he designed and made shoes for the wives of dignitaries in his home village of Bonito. Ferragamo came from humble beginnings and was one of 14 children. Over the twentieth century, his shoes became legendary, helped at the beginning by his move to the U.S. in 1914. He found a job in a shoe factory in Boston, but soon moved to be with his brothers in Santa Barbara, California, where he found work creating cowboy boots for the American Film Company. Ferragamo began to produce shoes for the silent-movie industry and became a success overnight. He was not just regarded as the shoemaker for the movies,

SALVATORE TAKES A FITTING, RIGHT. THE CLASSIC AUDREY PUMP, BELOW; STOCKING SHOES FOR FALL/WINTER 2000—2001, OPPOSITE LEFT

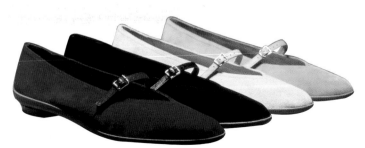

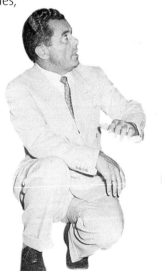

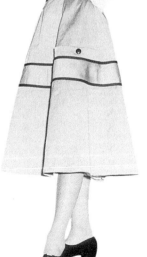

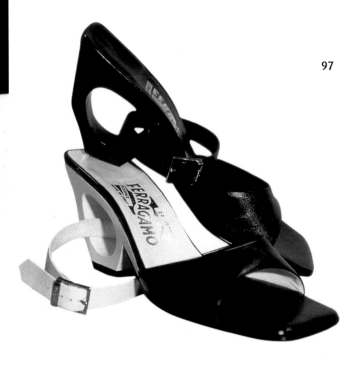

but for the stars personally as well. In 1928 he returned to Florence to sort out business at home, and he continued his work as shoemaker to the stars while expanding his business across Italy with stores from Milan to Naples. Word continued to spread about Ferragamo's genius for creating innovative shapes and using exotic materials, including python skin and gold, while guaranteeing that

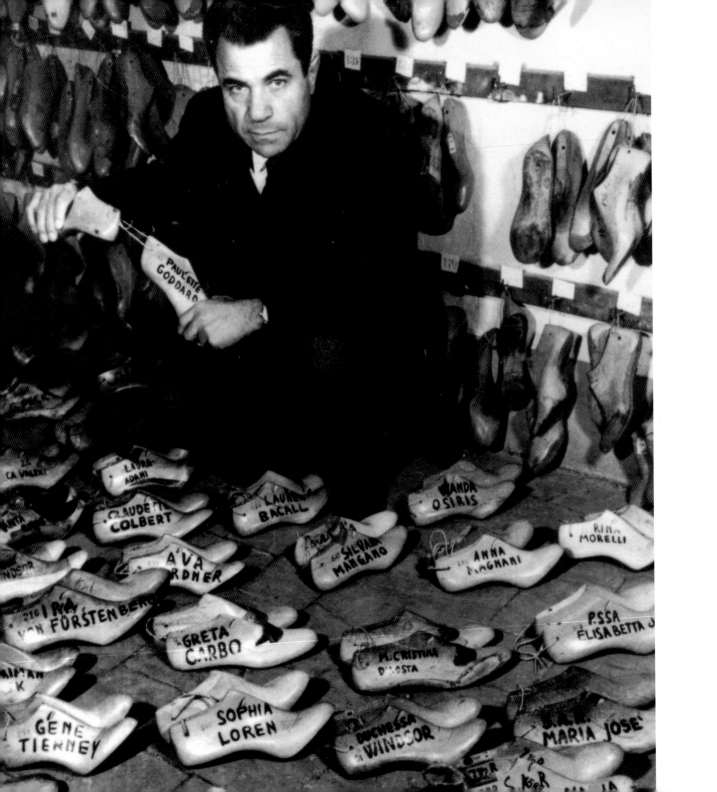

the shoes achieved perfection as regards comfort and fit. In addition to Gloria Swanson, Greta Garbo, Audrey Hepburn, Marilyn Monroe, and Katharine Hepburn, Ferragamo also made shoes for the Duchess of Windsor and the cream of high society in Europe. They loved his fine mix of artistry and craftsmanship, and his constant stream of fresh ideas—from wedges to "invisible" sandals held in place by invisible thread, deconstructed stilettos, odd-shaped heels, platform soles of cork or Bakelite, flat lace-ups for everyday wear, his use of raffia for sandals and intricate embroidery on evening shoes. He was truly a magician. Ferragamo died in 1960, but his wife Wanda and their children kept the business, expanding into fashion and handbags. For fall/winter 2000—2001, the house revived the classic Ferragamo wedge and the Monroe shoe has been reproduced as a special edition.

THE **FERRAGAMO** LEGACY SPANS TWO DECADES DURING WHICH THE DESIGNER BECAME SHOEMAKER TO THE STARS

FREE LANCE

French company Free Lance is also a family business. It was created by the Rautureau brothers and established by their grandfather in La Gaubretiere, northern France in 1870. Over a century later, Guy and Yvon continue to produce their shoes in the same factory.

In addition to its own collections, including two other brands, No Name and Pom d'Api, Free Lance has worked with designer Boudicca and Marcus Constable in London, as well as with John Galliano and Martine Sitbon in Paris. There are stores worldwide, including London, Los Angeles, Tokyo, and New York. Clients include Madonna, Cindy Crawford, Yasmin Le Bon, Kylie Minogue, Beth Orton, and the All Saints. Plans are afoot for a couture boutique in London's Soho to bring the celebrity service to anyone able to afford it.

FREE LANCE SHOES ARE OUT THERE—GLAMOROUS, SEXY, AND AT THE FOREFRONT OF FASHION

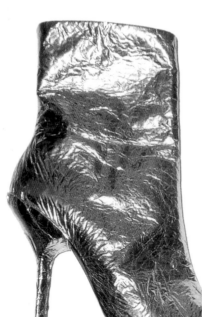

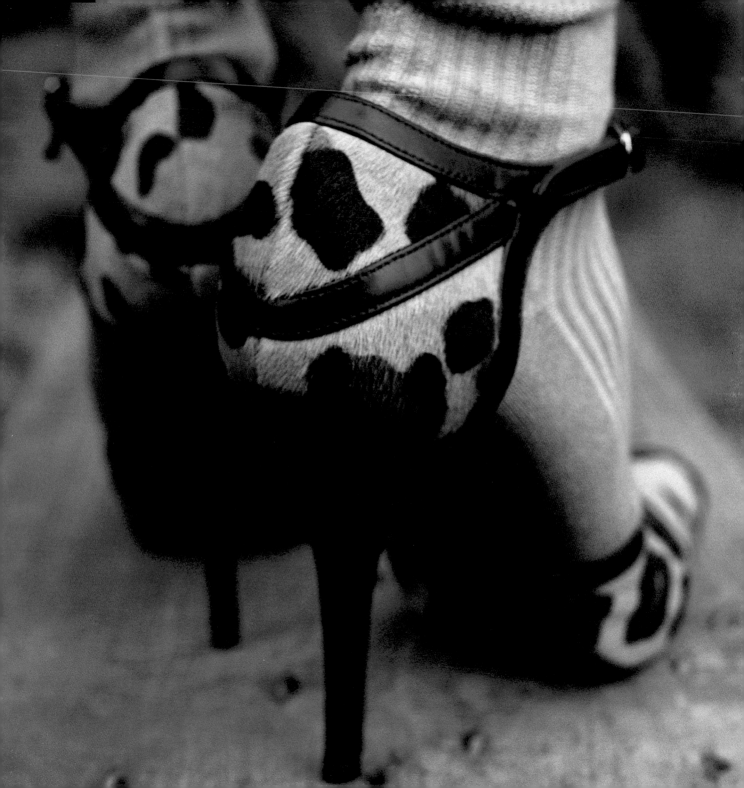

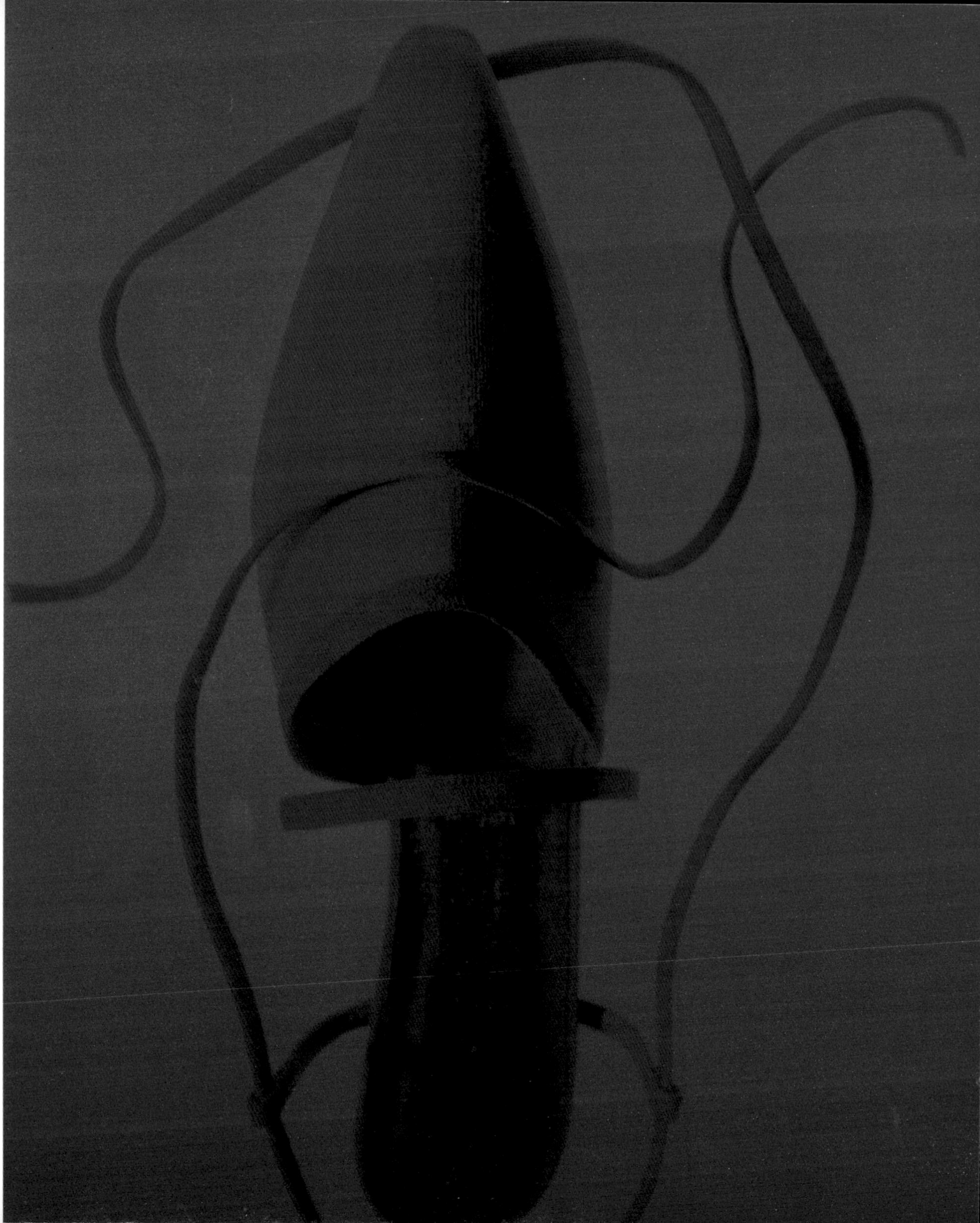

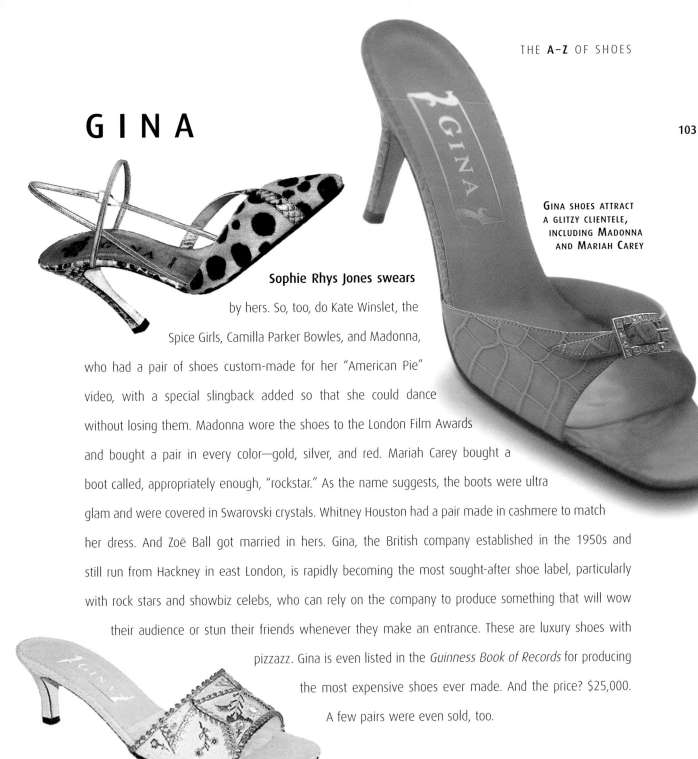

GINA

GINA SHOES ATTRACT
A GLITZY CLIENTELE,
INCLUDING MADONNA
AND MARIAH CAREY

Sophie Rhys Jones swears

by hers. So, too, do Kate Winslet, the

Spice Girls, Camilla Parker Bowles, and Madonna,

who had a pair of shoes custom-made for her "American Pie"

video, with a special slingback added so that she could dance

without losing them. Madonna wore the shoes to the London Film Awards

and bought a pair in every color—gold, silver, and red. Mariah Carey bought a

boot called, appropriately enough, "rockstar." As the name suggests, the boots were ultra

glam and were covered in Swarovski crystals. Whitney Houston had a pair made in cashmere to match

her dress. And Zoë Ball got married in hers. Gina, the British company established in the 1950s and

still run from Hackney in east London, is rapidly becoming the most sought-after shoe label, particularly

with rock stars and showbiz celebs, who can rely on the company to produce something that will wow

their audience or stun their friends whenever they make an entrance. These are luxury shoes with

pizzazz. Gina is even listed in the *Guinness Book of Records* for producing

the most expensive shoes ever made. And the price? $25,000.

A few pairs were even sold, too.

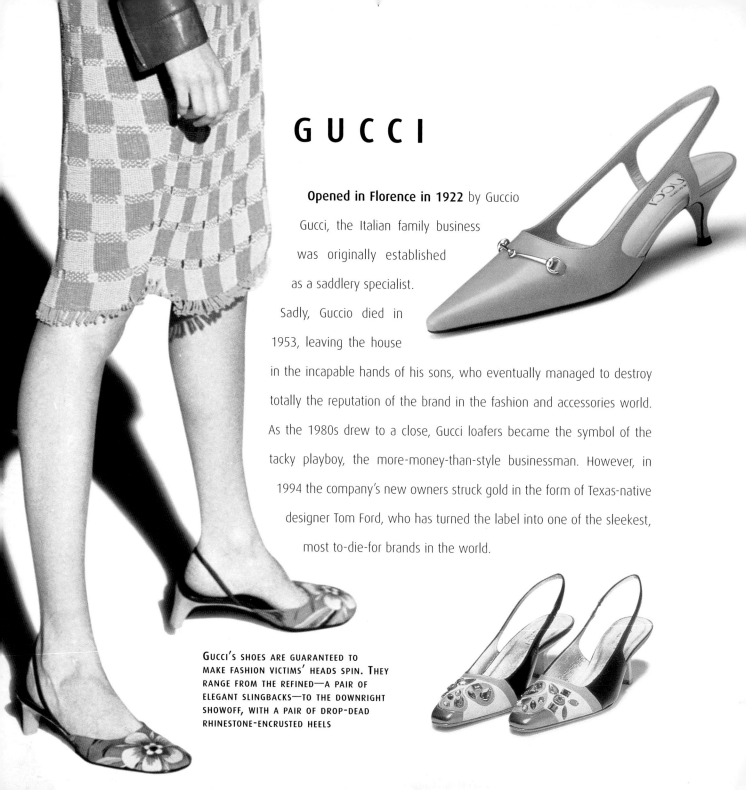

GUCCI

Opened in Florence in 1922 by Guccio Gucci, the Italian family business was originally established as a saddlery specialist. Sadly, Guccio died in 1953, leaving the house in the incapable hands of his sons, who eventually managed to destroy totally the reputation of the brand in the fashion and accessories world. As the 1980s drew to a close, Gucci loafers became the symbol of the tacky playboy, the more-money-than-style businessman. However, in 1994 the company's new owners struck gold in the form of Texas-native designer Tom Ford, who has turned the label into one of the sleekest, most to-die-for brands in the world.

GUCCI'S SHOES ARE GUARANTEED TO MAKE FASHION VICTIMS' HEADS SPIN. THEY RANGE FROM THE REFINED—A PAIR OF ELEGANT SLINGBACKS—TO THE DOWNRIGHT SHOWOFF, WITH A PAIR OF DROP-DEAD RHINESTONE-ENCRUSTED HEELS

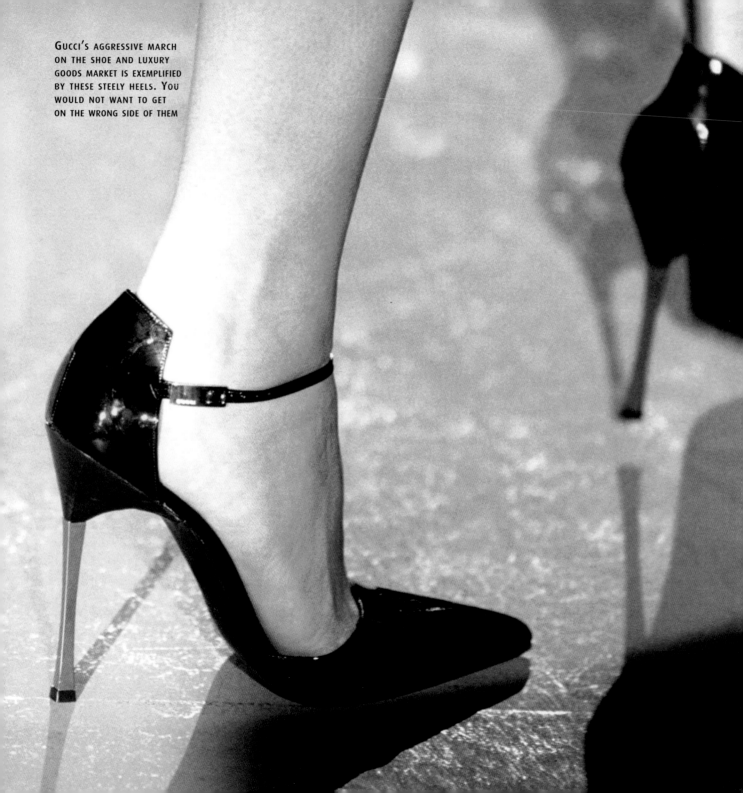

GUCCI'S AGGRESSIVE MARCH ON THE SHOE AND LUXURY GOODS MARKET IS EXEMPLIFIED BY THESE STEELY HEELS. YOU WOULD NOT WANT TO GET ON THE WRONG SIDE OF THEM

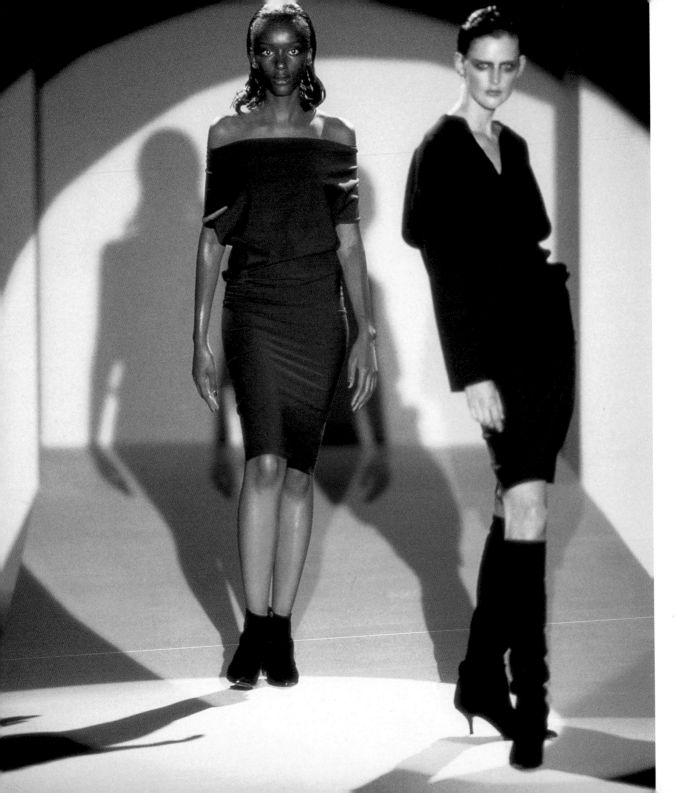

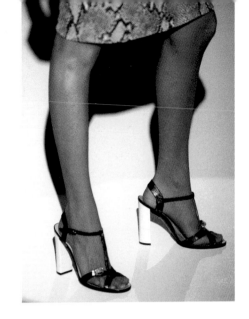

Ford looked back through the archives for inspiration and then reinvented the Gucci myth in the areas of fashion, fragrance, and, of course, the celebrated handbags. However, it is the shoe department of the store on Milan's

WHATEVER APPEARS ON THE GUCCI CATWALK TWICE A YEAR IS SURE TO ATTRACT RIP-OFFS ACROSS THE STREET. FOR TRUE GUCCI GALS, HOWEVER, ONLY THE REAL THING WILL DO

via Montenapoleone that is raided by a plague of fashion locusts twice a year during the Milan collections, when the fashion world stocks up on the coming season's slingbacks, spikes, and sandals. Gucci's waiting lists are legendary. There were the car-finish patent pumps, and then there were the crocodile slingback pointies that brought fashion followers out in a cold sweat. Most recently, Gucci's high-flyers have included a slinky pair of beaded, feathered slingbacks, with a low kitten heel made of bright turquoise plastic, and ruched velvet boots guaranteed to make their wearer feel just like a rock star.

EMMA HOPE

She calls her shoes "regalia for feet." Certainly, "shoes" seems far too mundane a word to describe Emma Hope's flights of fancy. Emma Hope Shoes was first established in 1985, shortly after the designer graduated from Cordwainers College. The following year she opened a store in Islington, north London, where she also chose to base her studio. Right from the beginning, Hope's shop was a popular destination for all shoe enthusiasts, especially those on a mission to find the perfect pair of wedding shoes. Her fine pastel-colored

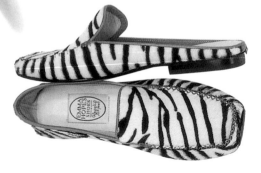

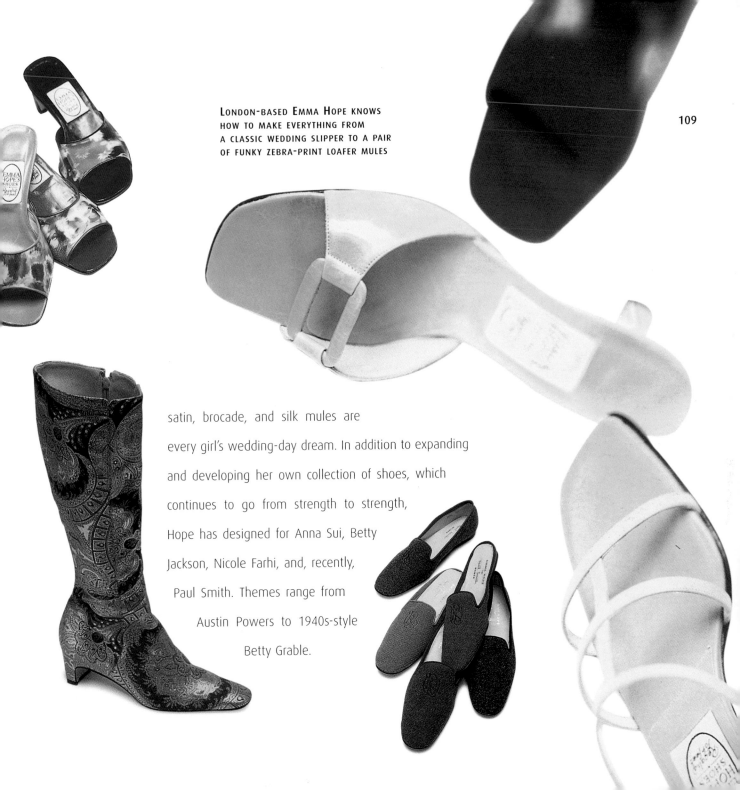

LONDON-BASED EMMA HOPE KNOWS
HOW TO MAKE EVERYTHING FROM
A CLASSIC WEDDING SLIPPER TO A PAIR
OF FUNKY ZEBRA-PRINT LOAFER MULES

satin, brocade, and silk mules are

every girl's wedding-day dream. In addition to expanding

and developing her own collection of shoes, which

continues to go from strength to strength,

Hope has designed for Anna Sui, Betty

Jackson, Nicole Farhi, and, recently,

Paul Smith. Themes range from

Austin Powers to 1940s-style

Betty Grable.

CHARLES JOURDAN

The Charles Jourdan name was created in 1921, but did not become fashionable until the 1950s, when the first Parisian store opened. The company is based in the Vercors mountain range of France, where plentiful water makes the perfect manufacturing base for leather goods; thanks to Charles Jourdan, it has become the manufacturing capital for luxury footwear.

Each pair of shoes is treated in its own right and undergoes almost 200 different processes, from the cutting of the leather to the stitching and finishing of the upper shoe. Charles Jourdan shoes are designed for women who like an arch in their foot and a reasonable heel; women who seek glamour, rather than practicality.

CHARLES JOURDAN'S SHOES ARE THE ESSENCE OF FRENCH CHIC, WITH PERFECTLY JUDGED HEELS AND FEMININE DETAILS

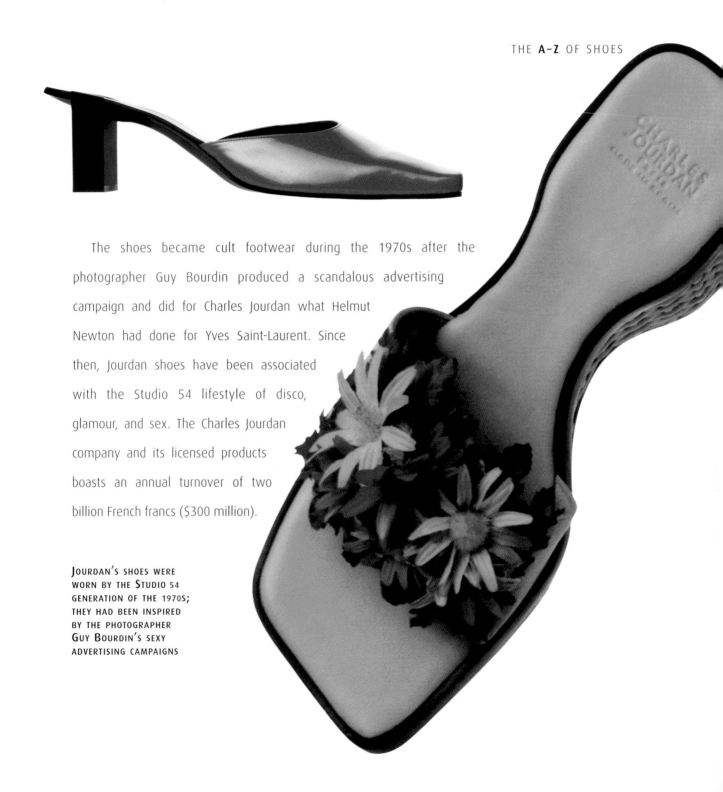

The shoes became cult footwear during the 1970s after the photographer Guy Bourdin produced a scandalous advertising campaign and did for Charles Jourdan what Helmut Newton had done for Yves Saint-Laurent. Since then, Jourdan shoes have been associated with the Studio 54 lifestyle of disco, glamour, and sex. The Charles Jourdan company and its licensed products boasts an annual turnover of two billion French francs ($300 million).

JOURDAN'S SHOES WERE WORN BY THE STUDIO 54 GENERATION OF THE 1970S; THEY HAD BEEN INSPIRED BY THE PHOTOGRAPHER GUY BOURDIN'S SEXY ADVERTISING CAMPAIGNS

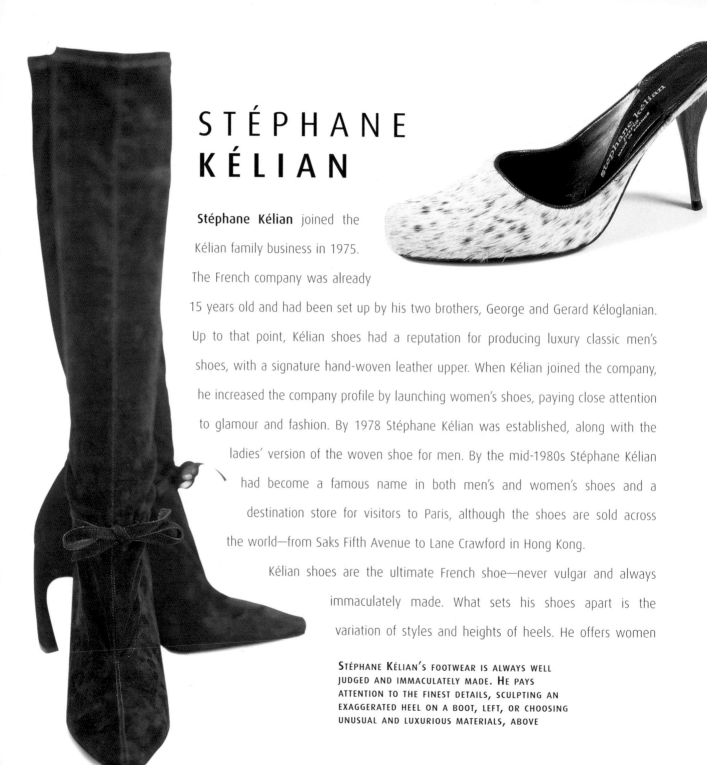

STÉPHANE KÉLIAN

Stéphane Kélian joined the Kélian family business in 1975. The French company was already 15 years old and had been set up by his two brothers, George and Gerard Kéloglanian. Up to that point, Kélian shoes had a reputation for producing luxury classic men's shoes, with a signature hand-woven leather upper. When Kélian joined the company, he increased the company profile by launching women's shoes, paying close attention to glamour and fashion. By 1978 Stéphane Kélian was established, along with the ladies' version of the woven shoe for men. By the mid-1980s Stéphane Kélian had become a famous name in both men's and women's shoes and a destination store for visitors to Paris, although the shoes are sold across the world—from Saks Fifth Avenue to Lane Crawford in Hong Kong.

Kélian shoes are the ultimate French shoe—never vulgar and always immaculately made. What sets his shoes apart is the variation of styles and heights of heels. He offers women

STÉPHANE KÉLIAN'S FOOTWEAR IS ALWAYS WELL JUDGED AND IMMACULATELY MADE. HE PAYS ATTENTION TO THE FINEST DETAILS, SCULPTING AN EXAGGERATED HEEL ON A BOOT, LEFT, OR CHOOSING UNUSUAL AND LUXURIOUS MATERIALS, ABOVE

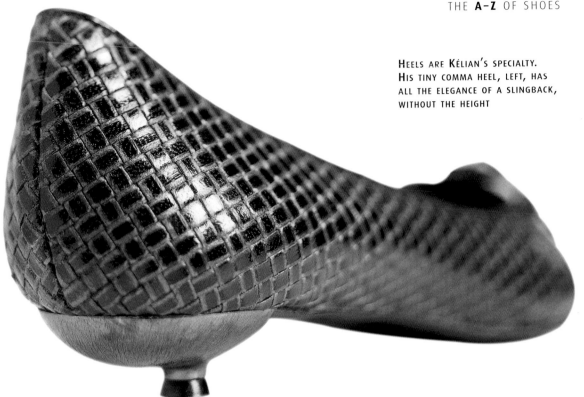

a choice, whether they are after something preppy or drop-dead sexy. A collection might include a pair of his "comma heel" kitten heels, an ankle strap thong, a rhinestone-encrusted satin stiletto, or a wedge which, he insists, always looks elegant and never chunky. The elusive combination of luxury, comfort, and style is key. His leather sandals, delicately embroidered with sprawling handwriting in gold thread, look as good on the foot as off it.

A SLINGBACK WEDGE,
RIGHT, IS A GOOD,
ALL-ROUND KÉLIAN CLASSIC

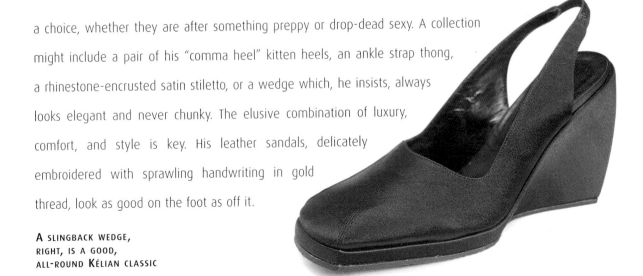

CHRISTIAN LOUBOUTIN

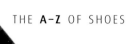

Christian Louboutin's shoes are very French and very feminine. Which is why women from Madison Avenue to Sloane Street love them. He started designing shoes for the stage—"Showgirls," he says, "are the best to design for because they wear nothing but a pair of shoes and a feather boa." Showgirls of another kind—Catherine Deneuve, Cher, Elizabeth Taylor, and Stella McCartney—all flock to Christian for their footwear needs, and especially for their footwear frivolities. "Chaussures are like a jewel," says the shoemaker who trained with Charles Jourdan. "It's the idea of pure luxury. If you offer a woman a beautiful ring, the magical moment is when she opens the box, Voila! I have to show my shoes in the same way." When the French film star Arielle Dombasle had a pair of shoes made for her by Louboutin, they came with a love letter from her husband locked into a see-through heel, along with a lock of his hair and a quill—the ultimate love token. Louboutin's shoes mix fantasy and art with romance, fashion, and craft. They are instantly recognizable from their bright red soles. As Louboutin himself says, "I like women to see my shoes as objects of beauty, as gems outside their own universe. Shoes are not an accessory; they're an attribute."

LOUBOUTIN'S SHOES ARE SEXY, COQUETTISH, AND VERY SHOWY. THE SOLES OF HIS SHOES, OPPOSITE, ARE A DISTINCTIVE RED

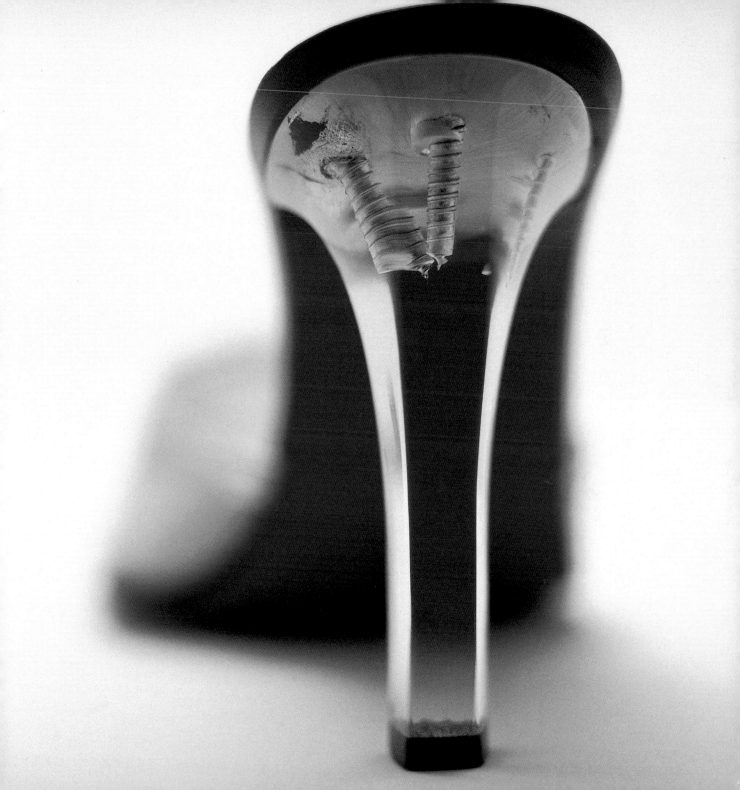

BENOIT MÉLÉARD

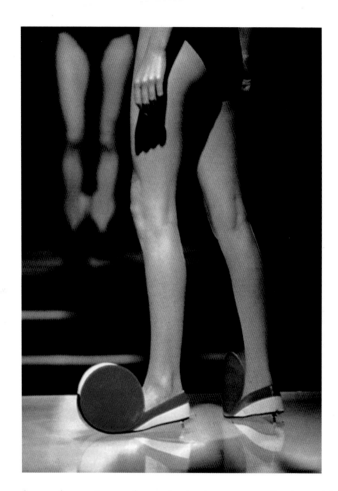

There is no getting away from it: Benoit Méléard produces shoes that are positively weird. Sometimes you would be hard pressed even to describe them as shoes. This is not surprising when you realize that the designer takes his inspiration from subjects like Leigh Bowery, the performance artist who was the life and soul of the London party scene throughout the 1980s, delighting friends and other revelers with his bizarre, comical, and often disturbing outfits. He was usually to be seen with orthopedic-looking wedges worn under tights, sometimes on just one foot. Méléard has created shoes for the young Paris-based designer Jeremy Scott, famously causing eyebrows to rise because one heel was higher than the other, making the models walk with an awkward gait. His other designs have included shoes without any soles or uppers whatsoever— simply a heel attached to the foot, leaving the rest of the shoe to the imagination.

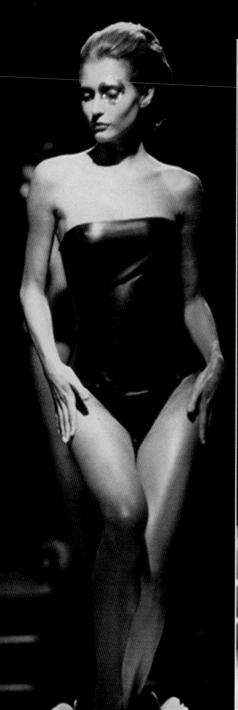

BENOIT MÉLÉARD CHALLENGES
THE WHOLE NOTION OF WHAT
A SHOE SHOULD LOOK LIKE   117

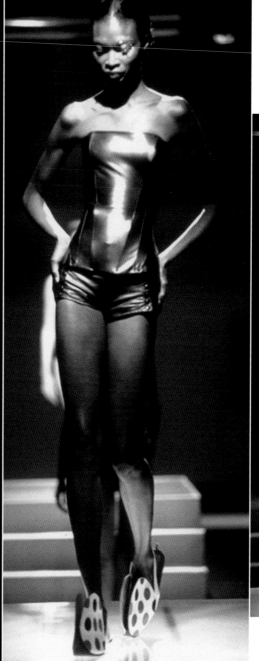

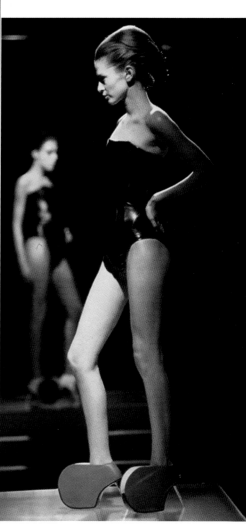

RODOLPHE MÉNUDIER

Born in 1961, the French shoe maestro Rodolphe Ménudier cannot remember a time when he did not feel passionate about shoes. Consequently, like many fashion designers, there was only one path his career could take. Ménudier has perfected both the art and the craft of the shoe. With his spindly, fragile heels, spiky metal stilettos, futuristic molded curves of Perspex and daring color palette, he is one of those designers who can make a girl melt. Aficionados love him. His shoes are sold in department stores like Harvey Nichols in London, as well as in some of the hippest boutiques, from Colette in Paris to Kirna Zabête in New York.

His first job after leaving college in 1986 was as house designer with Michel Perry. There, he developed the art of making a couture shoe, learnt business skills, and forged valuable contacts with couturiers with whom he has also worked—Paco Rabanne, Karl Lagerfeld (at both Chanel and Chloé), Balenciaga, and Christian Lacroix (for whom shoes are always high, elegant, and made in sumptuous shades of satin).

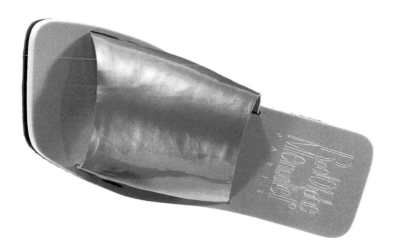

RODOLPHE MÉNUDIER IS THE FASHION EDITOR'S FAVORITE. THEY LOVE THE FRENCH DESIGNER'S RISQUÉ, SEXY SHOES, AND ENJOY HIS SENSE OF ADVENTURE, BE IT AN ELEGANT SLIPPER OR A DISCO DAZZLER WITH A PERSPEX SOLE AND GOLD STRAPS

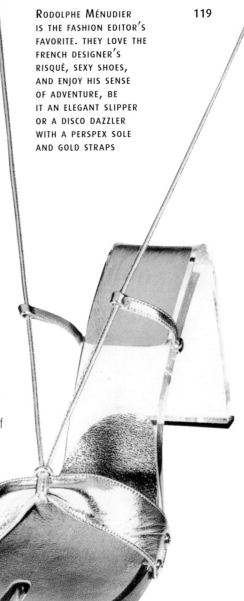

Every one of Ménudier's shoes is perfect, with the most beautiful balance of color, height, and detail, as befits the precise world of haute couture. With just six styles, he launched his own collection in 1994, which he called "haute couture high tech." His trademarks are innovation and a creative use of color and materials, as reflected in his sexy, zippered boots; in other words, footwear that gets a girl noticed. The shoes pictured here demonstrate his flexibility as a designer as well as his innate modernity. A beaded mule is finished with a clear Perspex heel like a block of ice, and a gold strappy sandal is given an innovative sole made from a single piece of Perspex, molded both to support and show off the foot.

The Ménudier headquarters are close to the Place des Victoires, in the second arrondissement in Paris. In the fall of 2000 he opened his first stand-alone store—two whole floors of Rodolphe Ménudier—in one of the city's chicest shopping areas. For many women, it is almost like entering the gates of heaven.

JOHNNY MOKE

A visit to London's King's Road would not be complete without a trip to World's End, and the shoe designer Johnny Moke. Certainly, whenever Cher or Madonna are in need of special footwear, they are guaranteed to drop in for a consultation. His celebrity clients also include Mick Jagger, Jack Nicholson, Gary Oldman, Tom Cruise, and Nicole Kidman. The store was opened in 1983, just three years after Moke had started to make shoes. Word soon spread, and fashion pundits, especially in the worlds of music and the media, deemed a pair of Johnny Moke shoes a must. Moke began by offering only a made-to-order service for men and women, and then expanded his business with a manufacturer in Italy. He has recently moved his ladies' shoes back to London, where he has reverted to the handmade service with which he started, offering a very personal and intimate service, and making shoes that fit every curve of the foot. His men's shoes, meanwhile, are made in Northampton. In

JOHNNY MOKE USES A WIDE AND EXOTIC RANGE OF MATERIALS FOR HIS SHOES AND SANDALS, INCLUDING TASSELS AND BROCADE

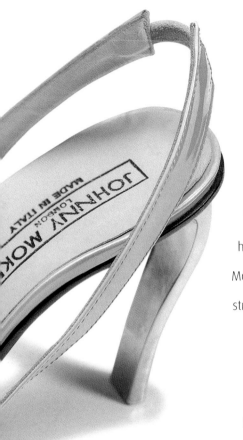

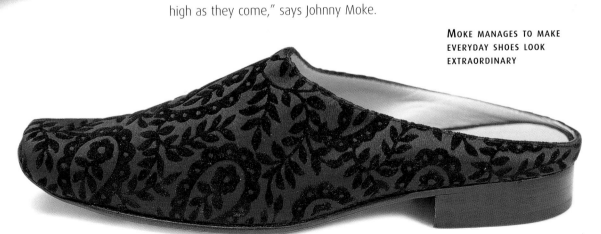

addition, he has taken the next logical step by extending his signature style into other areas—handbags, jewelery, belts, and other accessories.

Moke has one eye on classic shoe design and the other on London's street style, where the spirit of individuality still prevails. He likes to use baroque fabrics and color, print, and texture, but maintains that his shoes must display perfection in "form and shape." He describes his style and inspiration as a mixture of "street style with Savile Row, ethnic with Le Corbusier." And how do the likes of Madonna and Cher like their shoes? "As high as they come," says Johnny Moke.

MOKE MANAGES TO MAKE EVERYDAY SHOES LOOK EXTRAORDINARY

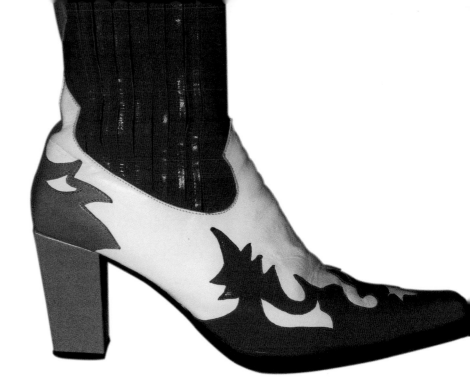

THERE IS SOMETHING ABOUT
THE SNUG FIT AND ELONGATED
CHISELED TOES OF MICHEL
PERRY'S BOOTS, COWBOY OR
OTHERWISE, THAT MAKES
THEM VERY SEDUCTIVE

MICHEL PERRY

Off the Place des Victoires in Paris, Michel Perry's shop is the essence of all that is French. The shop is all curlicues, delicate pinks, and pastel shades. It is as French as a madame's boudoir. In addition to shoes, there are clothes, hand-picked from various designers. But the women who make a pilgrimage to the shop each season—both at the beginning and at the end when the sale starts—are interested in only one thing: their feet.

Perry, who trained at the École des Beaux-Arts in the center of Paris, has been making shoes, boots, and delicate slippers since 1987. He can make a sensible Mary Jane shoe like no one else can, giving it his own special spin, with an accentuated arch to the foot and a heel so well defined that it offers both height and perfect balance. One season he painted a design onto the leather heel of one of his elongated

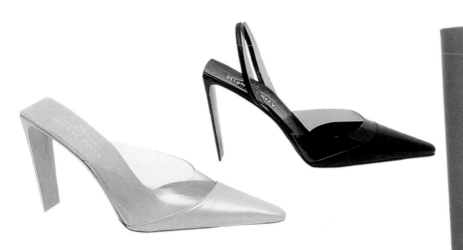

shoes. Another time, he let the supple kid leather speak for itself, leaving it completely plain, with just the tiniest of buckles fastening the shoe to the foot. The secret of his shoes—and what makes women come back for more, time and time again—is the long, pointy shapes that he has perfected, which make the feet look impossibly slender and feminine. There is something very sensual about having your foot zipped into a Michel Perry boot. It is enough to make a woman hand over her credit card without so much as checking the price.

Not only does he sell his own collection in exclusive stores around the world, from Barneys in New York to Harvey Nichols in Riyadh, Perry has also collaborated with several fashion designers on shoe designs for their own collections. Kostas Murkudis, Jean Colonna, and the young avant-garde talent Gaspard Yurkievich have all used his finely tuned eye to create exquisite footwear to complement their fashion fantasies.

124

PRADA

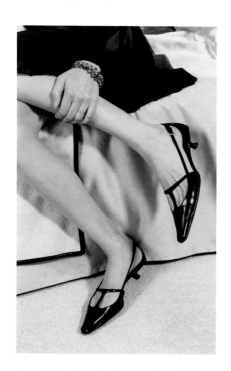

Just one red stripe is all it took, and the dedicated followers of fashion were at Miuccia Prada's feet. Literally. Prada, the family company founded in 1913 by Miuccia's grandfather Mario as a business making trunks and suitcases to order for wealthy Italians, has become the leader of all trends in shoes. What Miuccia puts on the catwalk in spring will be copied in the chains by summer, and stripped from the shelves as soon as stock arrives in Prada boutiques around the world. The great Prada renaissance was brought about by a

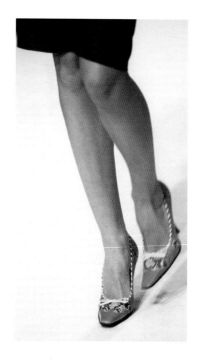

simple black nylon bag with a black-and-gold triangular logo. But it has been sustained by a clever strategy: seducing women at their most vulnerable point—their feet. Every season, the fashion pack take their seats at the Prada show in the tiny Milan catwalk theater, and wait with bated breath. It's not so much the clothes they want to see, but the shoes. They are even highlighted on an easy-to-view video screen so that anyone in the back rows can have a closer look.

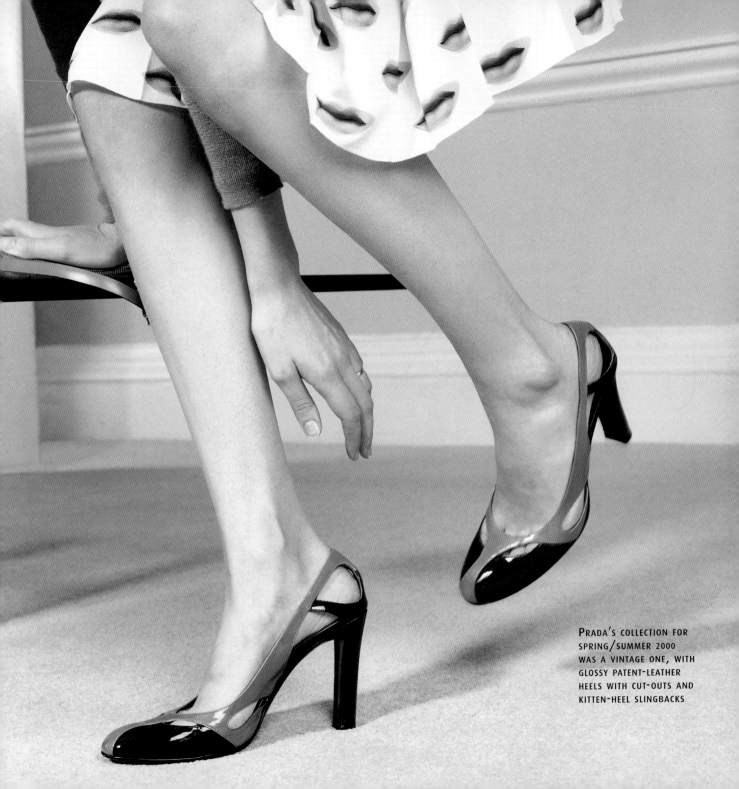

PRADA'S COLLECTION FOR
SPRING/SUMMER 2000
WAS A VINTAGE ONE, WITH
GLOSSY PATENT-LEATHER
HEELS WITH CUT-OUTS AND
KITTEN-HEEL SLINGBACKS

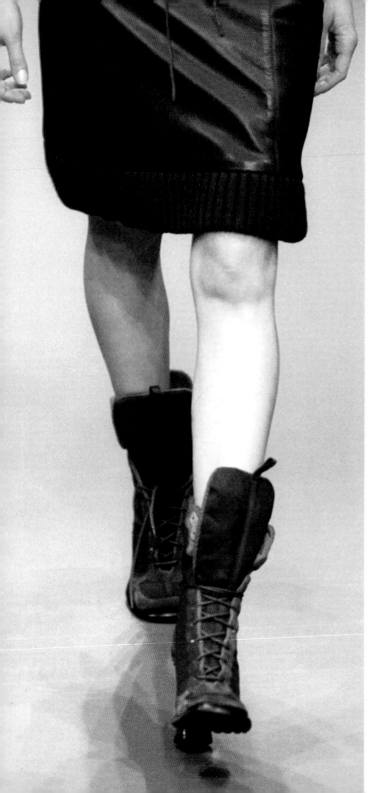

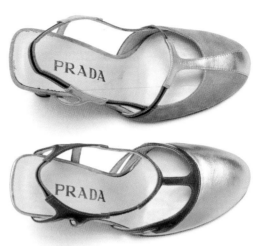

And although they are working, putting together trends, news stories, and ideas for shoots for the season ahead, they cannot resist making a mental shopping list. Because it's guaranteed there will be a shoe here that will keep them awake at night; they will not be able to rest until they are wearing it. From the Prada main line, there have been bestsellers like the Mary Janes with appliquéd leather leaves sprouting all over them; 1930s silver-screen-goddess shoes with chunky gold heels and Art Deco styling; sweet little mules with a bow at the front and a kitten heel; red-and-white patent-leather 1960s-inspired Mod shoes; and sporty trainer-style slip-ons, in iridescent blue or pink. Every shoe is a statement. And Miuccia knows how to strike just the right chord. Then there is Miu Miu, the more accessible younger sister line to Prada, featuring cowhide mules and shoes with molded heels, neoprene uppers, and fluorescent heels. And most recently, Prada Sport has been launched, the collection of aerodynamic trainers, sporty (rather than sports) shoes, and toggle boots that has made a simple red stripe into the ultimate status symbol . In fashion, they are all, quite simply, "to die for."

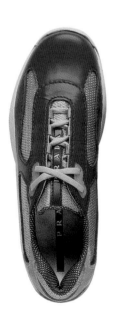

MIUCCIA PRADA'S SHOES RANGE FROM FUN TO FUNCTIONAL. SPORTS INFLUENCES ARE EVIDENT IN THIS HYBRID TRAINER BOOT (OPPOSITE, LEFT); STRAPPY LEATHER AND SUEDE SANDALS ARE GIVEN A MODERN EDGE WITH A STRIPE OF SPORTY ELASTIC (OPPOSITE, RIGHT); PRADA SPORT TRAINERS ARE AS FASHIONABLE AS THEY ARE FUNCTIONAL (LEFT); SISTER LINE MIU MIU IS YOUNGER AND MORE FRIVOLOUS—THESE JUMBO SEQUIN CIRCUS SHOES ARE A CLASSIC EXAMPLE (RIGHT)

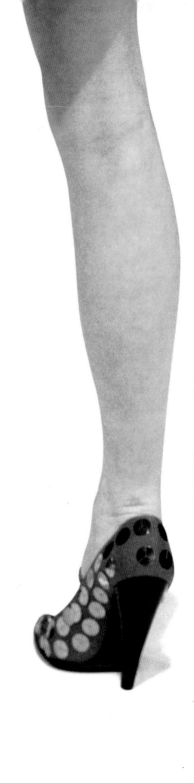

128

RED OR DEAD

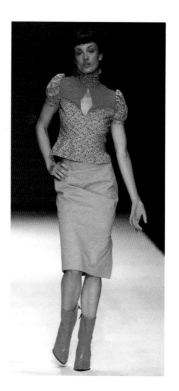

Wayne and Gerardine Hemingway are the sometimes warped minds behind Red or Dead, the company that began life in 1982 as a stall in Camden Market, selling secondhand clothing and footwear. They were hugely influential in the 1980s, both for their own shoe designs and for their idea to introduce Dr. Martens work boots as part of their stock. Jean-Paul Gaultier bought them from the Red or Dead market stall, and they became an icon of the 1980s, worn by everyone from Sade to Demi Moore. Red or Dead's own designs hit the spot, too; from the 1987 Watch Shoe—a chunky, ripple-soled lace-up that fastened with a wristwatch as a buckle—which sold out after boy band Bros took to wearing them wherever they went, to the 1990 Space Baby collection that featured a picture of a baby's head in an astronaut's

DISCO GLITTER MULES ARE
TYPICAL OF RED OR DEAD'S
GOODTIME ATTITUDE

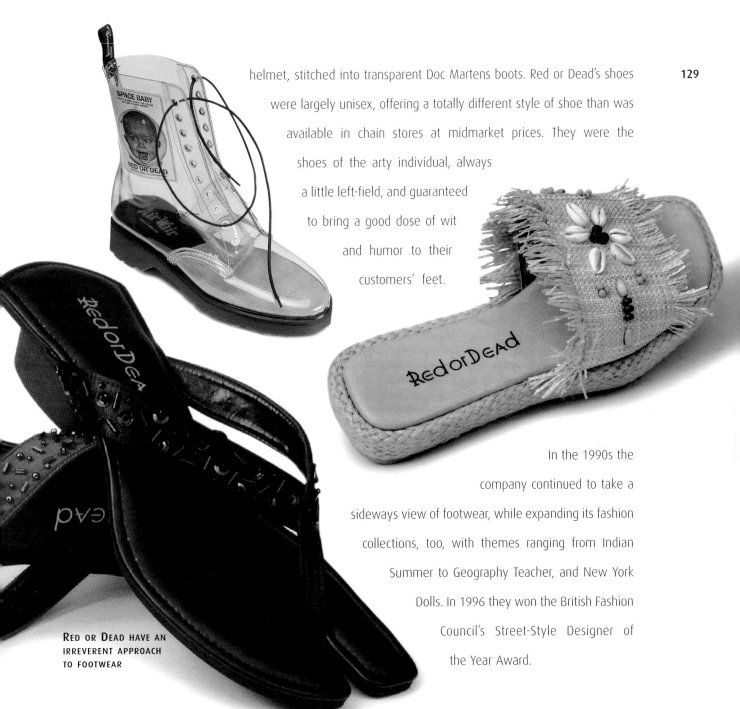

helmet, stitched into transparent Doc Martens boots. Red or Dead's shoes were largely unisex, offering a totally different style of shoe than was available in chain stores at midmarket prices. They were the shoes of the arty individual, always a little left-field, and guaranteed to bring a good dose of wit and humor to their customers' feet.

In the 1990s the company continued to take a sideways view of footwear, while expanding its fashion collections, too, with themes ranging from Indian Summer to Geography Teacher, and New York Dolls. In 1996 they won the British Fashion Council's Street-Style Designer of the Year Award.

RED OR DEAD HAVE AN IRREVERENT APPROACH TO FOOTWEAR

SERGIO ROSSI

It is no wonder that Gucci chose to buy a 70 percent stake in Sergio Rossi in November 1999. In the world's most fashionable circles, Rossi's super-sexy high heels were giving Gucci's own designs a run for their money. (Not literally, of course; these shoes are not intended to be worn for running anywhere.) At the time, you could glance along the front row of any fashion show in Milan, and there would be as many Rossis dangling elegantly from the feet of the fashion cognoscenti as Guccis and Pradas. Located on Milan's chic via Montenapoleone, the store would be constantly packed with fashionistas competing for the highest, strappiest heels. These are shoes designed for making an entrance; the more flirtatious and brighter the better. Risky heels for risqué women. Shoes that spell sex.

Only a man could be responsible for such high-voltage footwear, and when Rossi first began designing shoes as a young boy in San Mauro Pascoli in the 1950s, he should really have been questioned as to the purity of his thoughts. His father had crafted made-to-measure shoes before him, and that

SERGIO ROSSI'S
LEAF SHOE, LEFT, FROM
HIS COLLECTION FOR
SPRING/SUMMER 2000

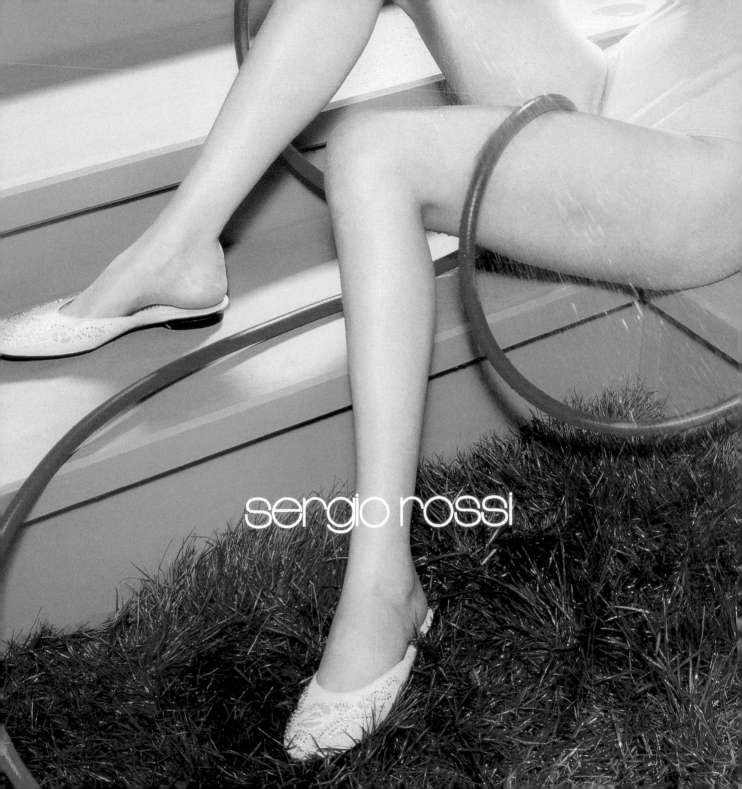

sergio rossi

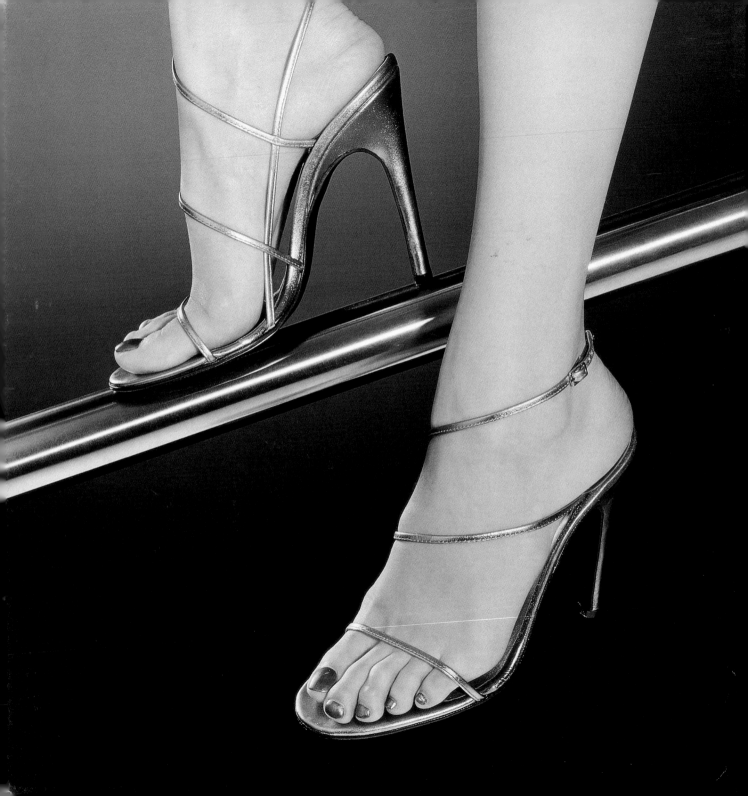

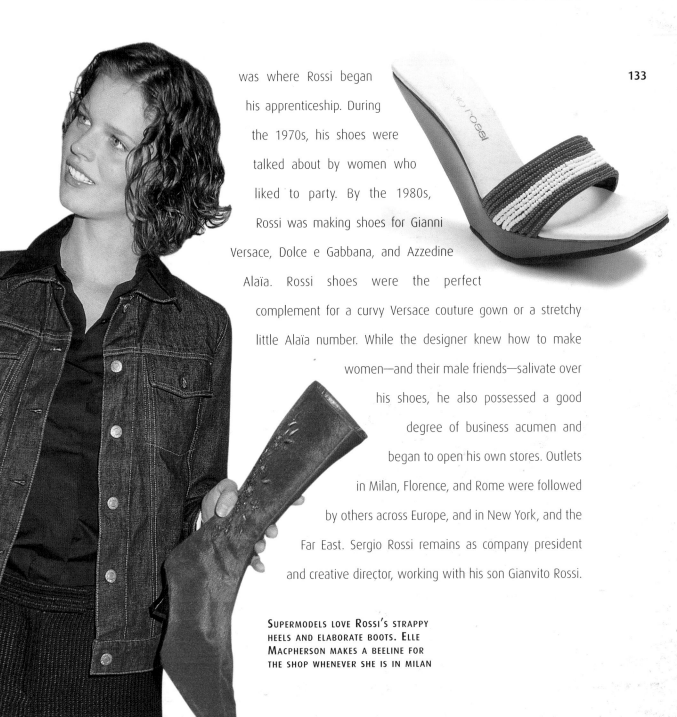

was where Rossi began his apprenticeship. During the 1970s, his shoes were talked about by women who liked to party. By the 1980s, Rossi was making shoes for Gianni Versace, Dolce e Gabbana, and Azzedine Alaïa. Rossi shoes were the perfect complement for a curvy Versace couture gown or a stretchy little Alaïa number. While the designer knew how to make women—and their male friends—salivate over his shoes, he also possessed a good degree of business acumen and began to open his own stores. Outlets in Milan, Florence, and Rome were followed by others across Europe, and in New York, and the Far East. Sergio Rossi remains as company president and creative director, working with his son Gianvito Rossi.

SUPERMODELS LOVE ROSSI'S STRAPPY HEELS AND ELABORATE BOOTS. ELLE MACPHERSON MAKES A BEELINE FOR THE SHOP WHENEVER SHE IS IN MILAN

J P T O D

J P Tod's—or simply "Tod's" as they are known—are the off-duty shoes of the jet set. The Italian entrepreneur Diego della Valle first saw a gap in the market in the early 1980s, and, having stumbled across an intriguing vintage driving shoe, della Valle sent it to his father's shoe factory near Ancona and asked for it to be replicated. The design was a classic, but its marketing was pure genius. Almost 20 years later, Tod's is a major player in the Italian—indeed the international—luxury leather business, with an annual turnover of £110 million. And like the running shoe, the driving shoe, with the knobbly heel grip in rubber, is worn for everything but driving. "Tod's" are the South Kensington Sloane's shoe of choice,

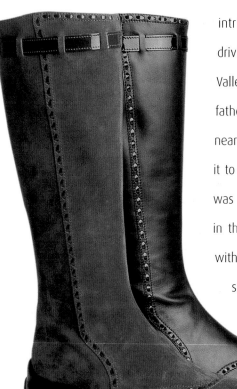

J P Tod's are the off-duty shoes of the jet set—comfortable, practical, and chic

and they are also sported by the Italian businesswoman on her travels, as well as the American fashion editor, who will most likely carry a pair of them in her bag at all times—for when the Manolos become too much to cope with. J P Tod's is a company with a century of family shoe-making behind it, and this is now combined with a design and marketing expertise that keeps the brand both forward-looking and in demand.

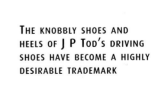

THE KNOBBLY SHOES AND HEELS OF J P TOD'S DRIVING SHOES HAVE BECOME A HIGHLY DESIRABLE TRADEMARK

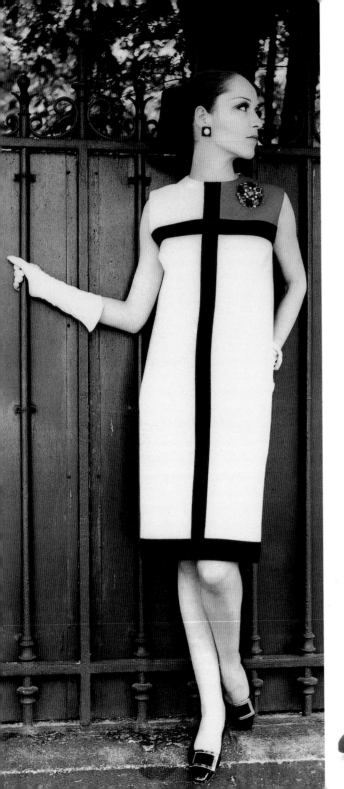

ROGER VIVIER

The man credited with inventing the stiletto heel in 1954—the shoe that so perfectly accentuated Christian Dior's revolutionary designs of that decade—was, not surprisingly, known as the Heel King. He designed Queen Elizabeth's shoes for her coronation in 1953. Only he could make the shoe look so regal—and so sexy—while making it comfortable and practical at the same time. The shoes featured a special double sole that gave the Queen— a size 37—extra height without her having to battle with a ridiculous heel. Vivier's shoes were the stuff of dreams. He preferred to call his creations *souliers*—more refined than the everyday *chaussures*—and, indeed, they were certainly anything but everyday. Roger Vivier is the couturier of the woman's foot; he is its milliner, its furrier,

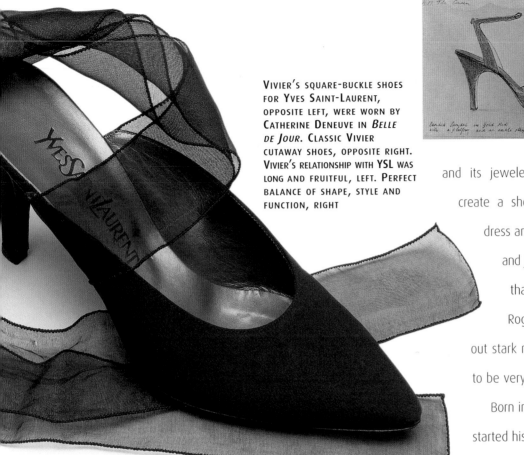

VIVIER'S SQUARE-BUCKLE SHOES FOR YVES SAINT-LAURENT, OPPOSITE LEFT, WERE WORN BY CATHERINE DENEUVE IN *BELLE DE JOUR.* CLASSIC VIVIER CUTAWAY SHOES, OPPOSITE RIGHT. VIVIER'S RELATIONSHIP WITH YSL WAS LONG AND FRUITFUL, LEFT. PERFECT BALANCE OF SHAPE, STYLE AND FUNCTION, RIGHT

and its jeweler. He manages to create a shoe that is at once dress and coat and hairstyle and jewelery, to the point that a woman shod by Roger Vivier who went out stark naked would appear to be very much dressed.

Born in Paris in 1907 Vivier started his apprenticeship as a bootmaker. He opened his first shop in Paris in 1937 in the ritzy rue Royale. During the war he set up shop in New York, until rations resulted in a ban on the making of new shoes. He reinvented himself as a milliner, but returned to his beloved shoes, and Paris, in time to work with Christian Dior and his New Look. In 1953 he began making shoes for Dior, and for the first time his shoes became—relatively—affordable and accessible to a wider audience. After Dior's death, Vivier designed for Yves Saint-Laurent's new label. Among his many innovations, he was the first to use see-through plastic. He continued working and innovating until his death at the age of 90 in 1998.

PAUL MURRAY WATSON

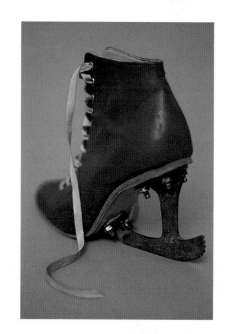

Young British shoe designer
Paul Murray Watson was first acclaimed for the shoes he designed for the avant-garde design duo Boudicca. They were a strange hybrid of high-heel boot and ice-skating shoe. Half an ice-skate blade was screwed into the sole of the elegant lace-up boot in place of a heel. The blades came from secondhand skates.

Murray Watson was born in Nottingham, in Britain's shoe-manufacturing heartland, and graduated from the Hand-sewn Shoe course at London's Cordwainers College in 1995. He immediately found work designing shoes and making lasts for various companies at home and abroad, proving that he could create shoes with mass-market and commercial appeal. Murray Watson now consults for shoe companies in Taiwan and Holland, at the

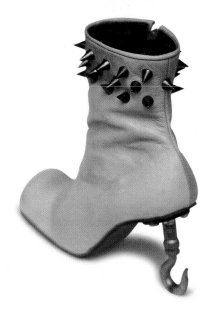

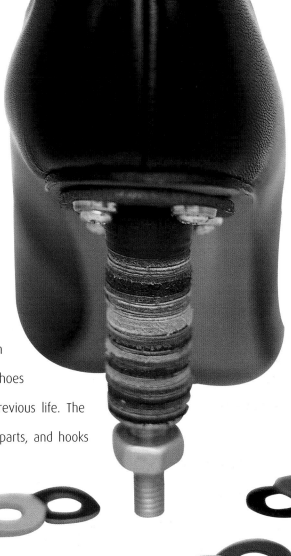

same time as expanding his own label and
designing shoes for Michiko Koshino, Tristan
Webber, Robert Carey Williams, and a young
British designer, Lizzy Disney, who showed
her collection for fall/winter 2000—2001 in
New York. He presented his first solo collection
at London Fashion Week in spring 2000, with shoes
that looked as though they had all had a previous life. The
designs make use of sculptured metal, BMX parts, and hooks
and screws. He describes them as "wearable
shoes as art."

**WATSON MAKES
SHOES AS ART,
USING RECYCLED
HOOKS, SCREWS,
AND ICE SKATES**

VIVIENNE WESTWOOD

She has always had a thing about shoes: from her swashbuckling pirates and buffalo girls of the early 1980s, to her rocking-horse shoes and gravity-defying platforms of the late 1990s, Vivienne Westwood's shoes have always been extraordinary. For fall/winter 1981—1982, there were pirate boots, all baggy around the ankles. In spring/summer 1985, Westwood fans were treated to platform shoes, designed to be worn with the "mini crini." By the following season, her shoes had become even more outrageous. Westwood called them "rocking-horse shoes." And they certainly rocked. Banana-shaped wooden platforms were tied to the leg, making running for a bus pretty impossible, although Westwood herself was spotted riding her bike in them. Others, including Westwood's friend and one-time assistant Jibby Beane, won't set foot outside in anything else; Japanese Westwood fanatics have long since

VIVIENNE WESTWOOD'S UNIQUE SHOES ARE ALWAYS EXTREME, WHETHER IN HEIGHT, STYLE, OR SUBJECT MATTER

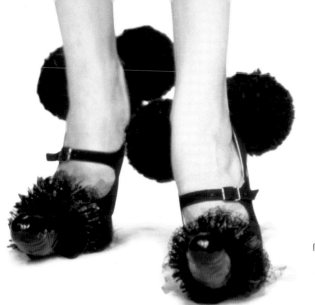

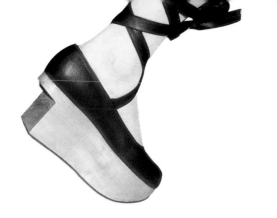

mastered the art of walking in Westwood platforms. By fall/winter 1990—1991, the shoes had grown in proportion to the Elevator platform, which, three collections later, had reached a dizzying ten inches in height. And then fashion history was made: Naomi Campbell fell off her platforms mid-sashay down the catwalk. Photographers snapped, and the audience clapped as she collapsed to the floor, smiled sweetly, and picked herself up like some graceful ballerina dancing in *Swan Lake*. It was a sensation, and newspapers worldwide lapped it up. The electric-blue snakeskin shoes took pride of place in the Costume Room at London's Victoria & Albert Museum on their own pedestal. Westwood knows how to create a drama.

WHEN NAOMI CAMPBELL FELL OFF HER ELEVATOR PLATFORMS, IT MADE NEWSPAPER HEADLINES

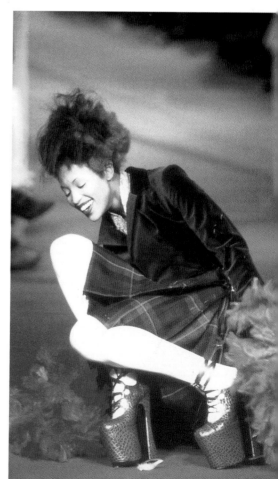

ADDRESS BOOK

Paul Andrew
Narciso Rodriguez's accessories
available at:
50 Bond Street
7th Floor
New York
NY 10012
212 677 2989

Birkenstock
Birkenstock.com
www.birkenstock.co.uk

Manolo Blahnik
13 West 54th Street
New York
NY 10012
212 582 3007

Camper
125 Prince Street
New York
NY 10012
212 358 1842

Chanel
9 West 57th Street
New York
NY 10019
212 688 5055

Jimmy Choo Couture
18 Connaught Street
London W2 2AF
44 020 7262 6888

Adele Clarke
Telephone 44 020 7916 4301
(general enquires)

Clarks
Available from stockists
Telephone 44 0990 785 886
(for stockist information)
www.clarks.com

Patrick Cox
4th Floor
Bloomingdales
1000 Third Avenue
New York
NY 10022
212 705 2000

Dolce & Gabbana
825 Maddison Avenue
New York
NY 10021
212 249 4100

Fendi
Harvey Nichols
109–25 Knightsbridge
London SW1X 7RJ
44 020 7629 5007

Ferragamo
661 5th Avenue
Trump Tower
New York
NY 10022
212 759 3822

Free Lance
235 King's Road
London SW3 5EL
44 020 7352 5731

Gina & Gina Couture
9 Old Bond Street
London W1X 3TA
44 020 7409 7090
www.ginashoes.com

Gucci
33 Old Bond Street
London W1X 3TA
44 020 7629 2716

Emma Hope
33 Amwell Street
London EC1R 1UR
44 020 7833 2367

Charles Jourdan
777 Maddison Avenue
New York
NY 10021
212 585 2238

Stéphane Kélian
717 Maddison Avenue
New York
NY 10021
212 980 1919

Christian Louboutin
941 Maddison Avenue
New York
NY 10021
212 396 1884

Doc Martins
1–44 King Street
London WC2 8HN
www.drmartins.com

Benoit Méléard
Made to order through:
Nicholas at Totem
33 1 49 23 79 76
www.benoit@meleard.com

Rodolphe Ménudier
Available at Harvey Nichols
109–25 Knightsbridge
London SW1X 7RJ
44 020 7584 0011

Johnny Moke
396 King's Road
London SW10 0LN
44 020 7351 2232
www.thebestofbritish.com

Paul Murray Watson
44 0973 740 854
44 020 8967 3255

Michel Perry
4 Rue de Petits Peres
Paris 75001
00 33 1 42 44 10 01

Prada
45 East 57th Street
New York
NY 10022
212 308 2332

Red or Dead
The Pentland Group
Pentland Centre
Lakeside
Squires Lane
London N3 2QL
44 020 8457 5005

Sergio Rossi
835 Maddison Avenue
New York
NY 10021
212 396 4814
www. sergiorossi.com

Dr. Scholl
Freephone 44 0800 074 2040

J P Tod's
41 East 57th Street
New York
NY 10033
212 644 5949

Vivienne Westwood
71 Greene Street
New York
NY 10012
212 334 5200

INDEX

ACKNOWLEDGMENTS

144

The publishers would like to thank the following sources for their kind permission to reproduce the pictures in this book:

t: top, b: bottom, l: left, r:right, tl: top left, tr: top right, bl: bottom left, br: bottom right, bc: bottom center, bcl: bottom center left, bcr: bottom center right.

Courtesy of Acupuncture 49
Miles Aldridge for Sergio Rossi 8–9, 10, 131–2
Robert Allan courtesy of Free Lance 14, 101
All Action/Jonathon Furniss 66tl
Courtesy of Paul Andrew (paulandrew@hotmail.com) for Yasmin Cho 74tr
Jibby Beane courtesy of Jonathon Gosland 32bl, 140–1b
Birkenstock courtesy of Modus Publicity 75bl, 75tl, 75cr
Courtesy of Manolo Blahnik 42, 79l/Manolo Blahnik for Antonio Berardi. Gold supplied by 'Chiampesan', Vicenza, Italy 27, 78
Simon Bower courtesy of Patrick Cox 51, 89bl, 91br, tl
© Buffalo Boots Ltd 33, 54–5
Paul Cahill courtesy of Patrick Cox 91tl
Courtesy of Camper 21br, 80–1
Pete Canning Photography for Clarks 87tl, 87tr, 87br
Courtesy of Chanel 82l, 83r
Jimmy Choo courtesy of Brower Lewis PR 84bl, 84l, 84–5c, 85r
Christie's Images Ltd 29, 58br
Corbis/Bettmann 20
Kevin Davies courtesy of Patrick Cox 89r
Courtesy of Dolce e Gabbana 94br
Graham Durridge courtesy of Gina 28, 103tr
Christopher Edwick for Free Lance 56, 70–1
Courtesy of Fendi Adele S.R.L./95/Karl Lagerfeld 95

Salvatore Ferragamo courtesy of Aurelia PR 26, 96, 97r, 98, 99br, 99tl, 144
Courtesy of Free Lance, Paris 100
Courtesy of Gina 102, 103 bl, tl
Giovanna courtesy of Patrick Cox 90tr
Ronald Grant Archive/*Batman Returns* Warner US 1992 40tr/*Barbarella* Panavision France/Italy 1967 41/*The Red Shoes* GFD/*The Archers* GB 1948 59/*How To Marry a Millionaire* TCF US 1953 60
Courtesy of Gucci 22, 47tl, 104br, 104tr, 106, 107bl
Courtesy of Hermès (GB) Ltd 36tr
Jürgen Holzenleuchter courtesy of Trippen, Germany 35bl, 53bl
Emma Hope courtesy of PH Publicity (photography by Ben Wright) 19br, 21tl, 108r, 109, 142–3/Paul Smith for Emma Hope 108l
Allen Jones *Shoes* (1968) 15r
Courtesy of Charles Jourdan 110–11
Ines Van Lamsweerde courtesy of Patrick Cox 72, 88
London Features International Ltd 34tl, 69/Dave Fisher 32r/Gie Knaeps 68l/George Pimintel 68br
Courtesy of Christian Louboutin 67br, 114–5
Niall McInerney 12t, 17, 37, 39r, 43, 82r, 83l, 140l, 141tr, 141br
Benoit Méléard courtesy of Girault-Totem PR, Paris 116–7
Courtesy of Rodolphe Ménudier 118–9
Christopher Moore Ltd 2, 15l, 16, 19tr, 24, 31, 35r, 52l, 58l, 77l, 79r, 86l, 90tl, 94tl, 94bl, 97l, 94bl, 104l, 105, 107tr, 124br, 126l, 127r, 128, 141tl
Sheridan Morley 38b
Chris Nash courtesy of No Name 44l, 45l
Courtesy of Nike UK 39tl/45br, 45tr, 46, 48
PA News Photo Library 35tl/William Conran 65c/Peter Jourdan 65tc/Neil Munns 64c/Stefan

Rousseau 65tr/John Stillwell 65l
Elaine Perks/Art Direction Mike Bond/Martin Coyne courtesy of As Øland 50l
Courtesy of Michel Perry 122–3
Courtesy of Prada 25, 44tr, 124tl, 125, 126tr/Alfredo Albertone 126tr, 127bl/Robert Wyatt 124tl, 125
Retna Pictures Ltd/Bill Davila 65br/Bukajlo/MPA 64tl/Soulla Petrou 89tl/Photofest 68tr/John Spellman 64tr, 64bl, 67r
Courtesy of Sergio Rossi 34br, 40–1c, 130, 133
Catherine Rowlands 12b/courtesy of Paul Murray Watson 138r, 139r/Bouddica 13, 138tl
Guy Ryecart courtesy of Patrick Cox 90bl
Jonathon Sands courtesy of Red Or Dead 128l ,128–9, 129tl, 129r
Dr. Scholl courtesy of SSL International 93
Matthew Shave 1, 47r
William Taylor courtesy of Adidas UK 36l/Paul Andrew for Yasmin Cho 74l/Manolo Blahnik 30, 76, 77r, 79l/Jimmy Choo 18/Adele Clarke for Hussein Chalayan 86br, tr/Patrick Cox 61/Fendi 23, 38t/R Griggs Group Ltd (Doc Martens AirWair) 92/Johnny Moke 120–1/As Øland 50r, 53tr/Red or Dead 129tl/Yves Saint Laurent 136br, 137l
Courtesy of Tod's 134–5
Topham Picturepoint 137r
Courtesy of Trippen, Germany 52–3t
Courtesy of Yves Saint Laurent/ (AW 1965) 136l

Every effort has been made to acknowledge correctly and contact the source and/or copyright holder of each picture, and Carlton Books Limited apologizes for any unintentional errors or omissions which will be corrected in future editions of this book.

Thank you to all the PR companies, fashion houses, and shoe designers who provided information and visuals for this book. Thanks to Ruth at Camper, Paula at Dolce e Gabbana, as well as to Sophia for always being high on heels, and to Jo for never letting a broken heel slow her down. I am also grateful to Venetia Penfold for her enthusiasm, Zia Mattocks for her patience, and to Barbara Zuñiga and Catherine Costelloe for their creativity and vision.

Tamsin Blanchard

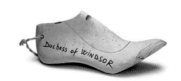